Complete ICT
for IGCSE®

Teacher Resource Kit

OXFORD
UNIVERSITY PRESS

Stephen Doyle

Great Clarendon Street, Oxford OX2 6DP

Oxford University Press is a department of the University of Oxford.
It furthers the University's objective of excellence in research, scholarship,
and education by publishing worldwide in

Oxford New York

Auckland Cape Town Dar es Salaam Hong Kong Karachi
Kuala Lumpur Madrid Melbourne Mexico City Nairobi
New Delhi Shanghai Taipei Toronto

With offices in

Argentina Austria Brazil Chile Czech Republic France Greece
Guatemala Hungary Italy Japan Poland Portugal Singapore
South Korea Switzerland Thailand Turkey Ukraine Vietnam

British Library Cataloguing in Publication Data

Data available

ISBN- 9780199129324

10 9 8 7 6 5 4 3 2 1

Printed in Great Britain by Bell and Bain Ltd, Glasgow

Paper used in the production of this book is a natural, recyclable product made from wood grown in sus-
tainable forests. The manufacturing process conforms to the environmental regulations of the country
of origin.

Acknowledgements

Cover image: Pasieka/Science Photo Library

p.6: 300dpi - Fotolia.com; **p.7**: Rob Byron - Fotolia.com; **p.7**: megasquib - Fotolia.com; **p.7**: Photosani - Fotolia.
com; **p.8**: luchshen - Fotolia.com; **p.8**: Juan Jose Gutierrez - Fotolia.com; **p.8**: Johanna Goodyear - Fotolia.
com; **p.9**: pressmaster - Fotolia.com; **p.9**: contrastwerkstatt - Fotolia.com; **p.18**: Korionov/Shutterstock;
p.18: Viktor Gmyria - Fotolia.com; **p.18**: Dragan Radojkovic - Fotolia.com; **p.19**: Stephen Coburn - Fotolia.
com; **p.19**: Haris Rauf - Fotolia.com; **p.19**: pressmaster - Fotolia.com; **p.20**: Tonis Pan - Fotolia.com;
p.20: Digital Vision/OUP; **p.20**: Supertrooper - Fotolia.com; **p.21**: tuja66 - Fotolia.com; **p.26**: Johnny Lye -
Fotolia.com; **p.26**: Allsop - Fotolia.com; **p.26**: Nikolai Sorokin - Fotolia.com; **p.27**: DLeonis - Fotolia.com;
p.27: Kevin Jarratt - Fotolia.com; **p.46**: V. Yakobchuk - Fotolia.com; **p.50**: vario images GmbH & Co.KG/Alamy;
p.50: With kind permission from Posturite; **p.51**: AlamyCelebrity/Alamy; **p.51**: With kind permission from
Posturite; **p.51**: Art Directors & TRIP/Alamy; **p.51**: Available from Barry Bennett; **p.61**: terex - Fotolia.com;
p.101: Piotr Rzeszutek - Fotolia.com

We have tried to trace and contact all copyright holders before publication. If notified the publishers
will be pleased to rectify any errors or omissions at the earliest opportunity.

® IGCSE is the registered trademark of University of Cambridge International Examinations.

University of Cambridge International Examinations bears no responsibility for the example answers to
questions taken from its past question papers which are contained in this publication.

Contents

Using the CD-ROM

Welcome to your *Complete ICT for Cambridge IGCSE® Teacher Kit*. The material on the CD-ROM has been prepared to help support your teaching. One these two pages you can see what you will find on the CD. Everything has been designed to help you prepare your students for success in this subject.

PowerPoint presentations

Customisable Powerpoints for each of the core content chapters help to summarize and explain topics.

Topic 7

Advantages and disadvantages of expert systems

Advantages

- Fewer mistakes - they do not forget things
- Less time to train - human experts take a long time to train
- More expertise than a single expert - systems based on expertise of many experts
- Always asks the questions that a human expert may forget to ask
- Cheaper - don't have the wage costs of a human expert

Disadvantages

- Systems lack common sense - they cannot spot a situation that is ridiculous
- Systems lack senses - for example, a patient may need to be observed
- The system relies on the rules being correct - the person creating the expert system may have made mistakes

Flexible digital support

All worksheets, activities and case studies in handy PDF and customisable Word format.

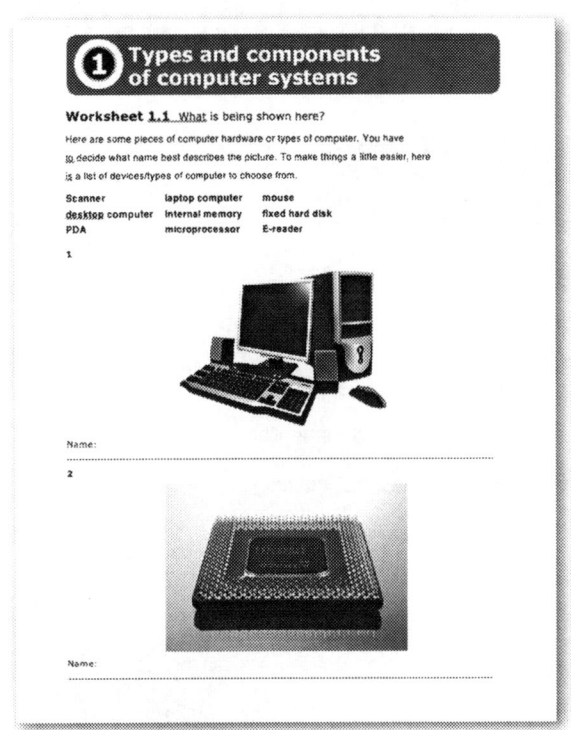

Mind maps and revision

Revision tools to support consolidation and exam preparation.

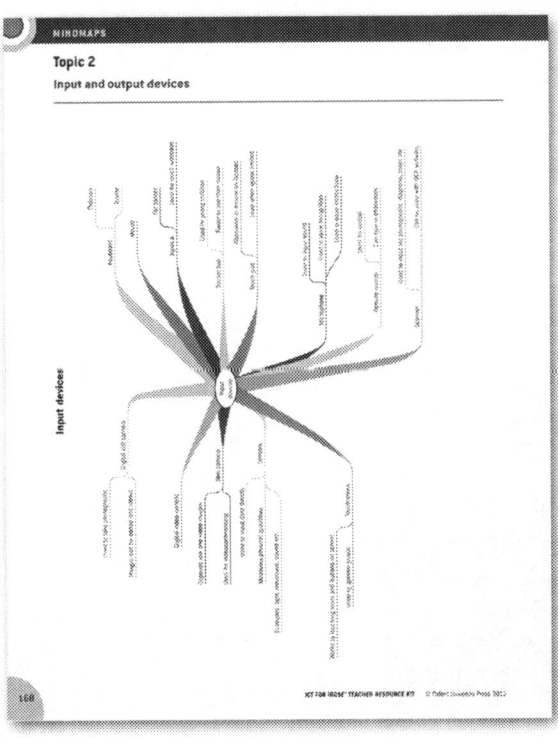

Activities data and documents

All the data to support the student activities in the *Complete ICT for IGCSE*® student book.

	A	B	C	D	E	F	G	H	I	J	K	L
1	Forename	Surname	Sex	DOB	No of IGC:	Includes N	Includes t	Position	Salary	Full or par	Driving licence held	
2	Yasmin	Singh	F	12/03/1992	3	Yes	Yes	Web desig	43000	F	Yes	
3	Mohamed	Bugalia	M	01/09/1987	10	Yes	Yes	Programm	48000	F	Yes	
4	Viveta	Karunakar	F	09/10/1978	5	Yes	Yes	Programm	16500	P	Yes	
5	Amor	Nanas	F	08/07/1987	6	No	Yes	Network e	67000	F	Yes	
6	Yuvraj	Singh	M	28/02/1990	11	Yes	Yes	Web desig	47000	F	Yes	
7	Sally	Sadik	F	12/03/1967	8	Yes	No	Programm	38000	F	Yes	
8	Mustafa	Karwad	M	01/02/1984	4	No	Yes	Systems a	54000	F	Yes	
9	Alex	Gomaz	M	30/09/1993	0	No	No	Artist	41000	F	Yes	
10	Bianca	Schastok	F	03/11/1980	0	No	No	Systems a	56500	F	Yes	
11	Vyoma	Pathak	F	14/12/1956	1	No	Yes	Technicia:	41000	F	No	
12	Nakul	Borade	M	22/06/1960	5	Yes	Yes	Web desig	45000	F	Yes	
13	Rachel	Liu	F	13/12/1961	7	Yes	Yes	Programm	38900	F	No	
14	Sho Ling	Wong	F	17/09/1978	9	Yes	Yes	Animator	28000	P	No	
15	Chloe	Burns	F	10/02/1972	5	No	Yes	Security a	52000	F	Yes	
16	Rachel	Hughes	F	16/09/1991	0	No	No	Network a	34200	P	No	
17	Grace	Hughes	F	25/12/1965	4	No	Yes	Director	78000	F	Yes	
18	Marzena	Jankowski	F	31/12/1955	2	No	Yes	Admin cle	32000	P	Yes	
19	Bishen	Singh	M	10/01/1950	0	No	No	Assistant	30500	F	No	
20	Raol	Ncube	M	12/01/1974	5	Yes	Yes	Director	87000	F	Yes	
21	James	Murphy	M	30/06/1964	4	No	Yes	Admin cle	26000	P	No	
22	Rajan	Uppal	M	22/08/1977	5	Yes	Yes	Web desig	14000	P	Yes	
23	Hamid	Zadeh	M	03/01/1992	10	Yes	Yes	Trainee ar	23000	F	Yes	
24	Kevin	Fortuni	M	30/09/1990	7	Yes	No	Trainee ar	26000	F	Yes	
25	Maria	Fortuni	F	16/06/1989	11	Yes	Yes	Technicia:	27000	F	No	
26	Rupinder	Singh	M	29/05/1990	6	Yes	No	Finance cl	24900	P	No	
27	Emily	Wilson	F	27/12/1989	4	Yes	No	Finance cl	37000	P	Yes	
28	Osama	Diad	M	03/11/1993	2	No	No	Trainee ne	23000	P	No	
29	Ahmed	Fathy	M	23/12/1990	7	Yes	Yes	Network e	41800	F	Yes	
30	Hassan	Sheata	M	09/11/1989	6	Yes	No	Network e	43000	F	Yes	
31	Abdullah	Nordin	M	02/01/1969	2	No	No	Web desig	42000	F	No	
32	Fay	Hoy	F	09/10/1988	8	Yes	Yes	Reception	21300	P	No	
33	Robert	Marley	M	17/05/1965	0	No	No	Marketing	21000	P	No	
34	Hassoune	Al Sheikh	M	01/01/1990	5	Yes	No	Marketing	27600	F	Yes	
35	Samantha	Jackson	F	09/12/1970	7	Yes	Yes	Programm	30500	F	Yes	
36	Mia	Hamm	M	06/11/1978	2	No	Yes	Finance cl	12000	P	No	
37												

1 Types and components of computer systems

Worksheet 1.1

What is being shown here?

Here are some pieces of computer hardware or types of computer. You have to decide what name best describes the picture. To make things a little easier, here is a list of devices/types of computer to choose from.

scanner	laptop computer	mouse
desktop computer	internal memory	fixed hard disk
PDA	microprocessor	E-reader

1

Name:

_____

2

Name:

_____

Worksheet 1.1 (continued)

3

Name:

_____

4

Name:

_____

5

Name:

_____

Worksheet 1.1 (continued)

Worksheet 1.1 (continued)

6

Name:

_____

7

Name:

_____

8

Name:

_____

Worksheet 1.1 (continued)

9

Name:

10

Name:

Worksheet 1.2

Hardware or software?

Here are some items that are either hardware or software. You have to decide which they are by putting a tick in the appropriate column.

	Name of item	Hardware	Software
1	Processor		
2	Operating system		
3	Fixed hard disk		
4	Memory chips (RAM and ROM)		
5	Keyboard		
6	Mouse		
7	Word-processor		
8	Search engine		
9	Speakers		
10	Microphone		
11	DVD drive		
12	Blank DVD		
13	Database		
14	Spreadsheet		
15	Bar code reader		
16	Printer		
17	Web browser		
18	Removable hard disk		
19	Wireless router		
20	Digital camera		

ICT FOR IGCSE® TEACHER RESOURCE KIT © Oxford University Press 2012

Activity 1.1

Wireless Internet

Many people who use the Internet do not want to be restricted by cables. They want to be able to access the Internet wirelessly wherever they are.

Imagine that you are employed in a job where you have a very busy schedule and have to do a lot of travelling.

For this activity you have to produce an advert which advertises a phone or notebook computer which can be used for Internet access. Your emphasis in your advert must be those features that will make the device as portable as possible and give very fast access to the Internet.

Make sure that your advert targets the busy person who is always on the move.

You are free to choose whatever software you think would be best for this task.

Topic 1 answers

Activity 1.1

Student book page 2

A typical list may include the following:

Keyboard

Mouse

Scanner

Touch screen

Microphone

Joystick

Remote control

Router

Pen/flash drive

Memory cards

Laser printer

Inkjet printer

Dot matrix printer

Processor

ROM/RAM

Web cam

Digital camera

Touchpad

Magnetic stripe reader

Chip reader and PIN pad

Graph plotter

Optical mark reader

Optical character reader

Bar code reader

Video camera

Light pen

Motor

Actuator

Fixed hard disk

Portable hard disk

Optical drive (CD, DVD, etc.)

Switch

Hub

Headphones

Activity 1.2

Student book page 2

Name of Item	Hardware	Software
Keyboard	√	
Operating system		√
Scanner	√	
Remote control	√	
Word-processor		√
Web browser		√
Mouse	√	
Spreadsheet		√
Database		√
DVD	√	
Laser printer	√	
Virus checker		√
CD-ROM	√	
Web design		√

Questions A

Student book page 4

1 a One mark for:

   Hardware – The physical parts of a computer that you can actually touch.

   One mark for:

   Software – The sets of instructions that you cannot touch that tell the hardware how to operate.

   b One mark for two examples of hardware such as:

   ▸▸ Keyboard

   ▸▸ Mouse

   ▸▸ Hard disk drive

   ▸▸ CD/DVD drive

   ▸▸ Internal memory (RAM and ROM)

   ▸▸ Screen

   ▸▸ Etc.

   One mark for two examples of software such as:

   ▸▸ Operating system/systems software

   ▸▸ Word-processing

   ▸▸ Database

   ▸▸ Spreadsheet

   ▸▸ Web browser

   ▸▸ Graphics

   ▸▸ Etc.

2 One mark for each:

A = Input devices

B = Processor and internal memory devices

C = Output devices

D = Secondary storage devices

3 a i Read only memory

ii Random access memory

b RAM

ROM

ROM

RAM

4 a One mark each for Read only memory and Random access memory.

b Any two answers (one each for ROM and RAM) similar to the following:

ROM is needed to store the program needed to boot the computer up.

ROM is used to hold the instructions to start the computer up.

ROM is used to give instructions to the computer to load up the operating system.

RAM is used to hold the program instructions currently being used.

RAM is used to hold the data currently being worked on.

5 a One mark each for two of the following:

Applications will run faster on their own.

More applications can be opened and run at the same time.

Users are able to move more quickly between applications.

b See answers to Question 4 (b).

Questions B

Student book page 9

1 a Any three from the following (one mark each):

Windows

Icons

Menus/Pull-down menus

Pointers

Online help/Office assistants

b One mark for one of the following:

Menu driven interface

Command line interface

Voice driven interface

Touch screen interface

2 a Two marks for two points similar to the following:

Programs used to control the hardware directly

Gives the step-by-step instructions to the hardware

Manages the system resources

b One mark each for three of the following:

Handles the inputs and outputs – controls the operation of input and output devices such as the keyboard, mouse, printer, screen, etc.

Recognizes hardware attached to the computer – recognizes that a device such as a pen drive has been attached and loads the software needed to control it.

Supervises the running of other programs – it provides a way for the applications software such as word-processing software to work with the hardware.

Handles the storage of data – decides where to store data on the memory and allows the user to create folders and sub-folders, etc.

Maximizes the use of computer memory – decides where in memory the program instructions are placed.

Handles the interrupts and decides what action to take – a paper jam will stop the printer and alert the user with a message on the screen.

Revision questions

Student book page 9

1 One mark for each difference to a maximum of two marks such as:

Desktop has a full-sized keyboard

Desktops sometimes have a larger screen

Desktops are meant to be used in one place

Laptops have keyboards and screen in one unit

Laptops are usually lighter

Laptops can be used with a portable power supply such as a battery

2 a One mark for:

Processes the raw data and turns it into information

b One mark for:

Stores program instructions and data that are needed immediately by the processor

c One mark for:

Used to hold programs and data that are needed instantly by the computer

Used for long term storage of programs and data

Used for backup copies in case the original data is damaged or lost

3 a One mark each for two input devices such as:

Keyboard

Mouse

Touch screen

Microphone

Bar code reader

Etc.

b One mark for two output devices such as:

Printer

Screen/monitor

Loudspeaker

Etc.

c One mark for two backing storage devices such as:

Magnetic hard drive

Magnetic floppy disk drive

Flash memory/pen drive

CD drive

DVD drive

Etc.

4 a One mark for each point to a maximum of three marks:

Desktop much larger in size or laptop much smaller

Desktop designed to be used in one place or laptop is portable

Desktop has full-sized screen/keyboard

Laptop is much lighter compared to a desktop

Laptop is sometimes operated by battery away from the mains power supply

b One mark for each point to a maximum of two marks:

Smaller than a laptop

Usually less memory

Mainly aimed at accessing the Internet

Does not usually have a CD/DVD drive to reduce weight

5 a One mark for Personal Digital Assistant.

b One mark for one of the following:

Can easily be used whilst standing up

Smaller and lighter means they can be put in your pocket

Less expensive to purchase

6 a One mark for each of two features such as:

Used to control huge networks of computers often located globally

Contain many processors enabling them to work on many jobs at the same time

Very large and need to have air-conditioning installed to cool them down

b One mark for each of two uses such as:

Processing the results of large scientific experiments

Processing large numbers of transactions such as bank transactions

Processing huge amounts of data needed to produce accurate weather forecasts

7 a You use two fingers with one finger moving up and the other moving down in order to rotate a digital photograph so that it is around the right way.

b You pinch your fingers together to zoom in or zoom out when viewing an image.

Test yourself

Student book page 10

A software

B hardware

C CPU

D software

E applications

F desktop

G input

H output

I ROM

J RAM

K ROM

L RAM

M pinching

Examination questions

Student book page 10

1 One mark each for the following items ringed:

Magnetic tape

Flash memory card

2 Any four of the following:

ROM is read only memory and RAM is random access memory

ROM is used to hold instructions to start the computer, which are called the boot program or BIOS (basic input/output system)

ROM is used to store data that cannot be altered by the user

RAM is used to store data that can be changed by the user

ROM is non-volatile memory because it does not lose its contents when the power is turned off

RAM is volatile because it loses its memory when the power is removed

RAM is read/write whereas ROM is read only

3 One mark each for the following items ringed:

Operating system

Web browser

4 One mark for each correct answer.

a Software

b Input

c Output

d ROM

e RAM

5 One mark each for any three of the following:

It recognises new hardware attached to the computer

Handles inputs and outputs

Supervises the running of other programs

Handles the storage of data

Maximises the use of computer memory

Handles interrupts and decides what to do

6 a Two advantages such as:

PDAs are smaller/lighter and are more portable

PDAs are easier to use whilst standing

Many can be used as a mobile phone which means that two separate devices are not needed

b Two disadvantages such as:

PDAs usually have smaller memory which limits the things they can do

PDAs are small and this can make it difficult for some users to use

PDAs are small and so are often lost

c One mark each for any three of the following:

Windows

Icons

Menus

Pointers

Worksheet: What is being shown here?

Teacher Resource Kit page 6

1 Desktop computer

2 Microprocessor

3 Fixed hard disk

4 Mouse

5 E-reader

6 Scanner

7 Internal memory

8 PDA

9 Laptop computer

10 Netbook computer

Worksheet 1.2: Hardware or software?

Teacher Resource Kit page 10

	Name of item	Hardware	Software
1	Processor	√	
2	Operating system		√
3	Fixed hard disk	√	
4	Memory chips (RAM and ROM)	√	
5	Keyboard	√	
6	Mouse	√	
7	Word-processor		√
8	Search engine		√
9	Speakers	√	
10	Microphone	√	
11	DVD drive	√	
12	Blank DVD	√	
13	Database		√
14	Spreadsheet		√
15	Bar code reader	√	
16	Printer	√	
17	Web browser		√
18	Removable hard disk	√	
19	Wireless router	√	
20	Digital camera	√	

2 Input and output devices

Worksheet 2.1

Can you work out what the word is?

Here are some words or phrases which have been jumbled up. The words are connected with input or output devices. Can you work out what they are? There is a clue to help you.

1 Cab mew

Hint: You can see who you are chatting to with one of these.

Answer: _____

2 Res sons

Hint: Temperature data can come from these.

Answer: _____

3 Use om

Hint: Very popular input device which can be wired or wireless.

Answer: _____

4 Niche promo

Hint: You enter data by speaking into one of these.

Answer: _____

5 Narcs en

Hint: Useful for capturing old photographs so they can be stored on a computer.

Answer: _____

6 Broad key

Hint: Almost every computer comes with one of these input devices.

Answer: _____

ICT FOR IGCSE® TEACHER RESOURCE KIT   © Oxford University Press 2012

Worksheet 2.1 (continued)

7 **Tick joys**

Hint: One of these is useful for playing games.

Answer: _____

8 **Tripes**

Hint: You get a magnetic one of these on a credit card.

Answer: _____

9 **Creative nit**

Hint: An _____ whiteboard.

Answer: _____

10 **Crag ship**

Hint: A _____ tablet used as an input device.

Answer: _____

Worksheet 2.2

Can you name the input or output devices shown?

Give the name of the input or output device shown.

1

Name:

_____

2

Name:

_____

3

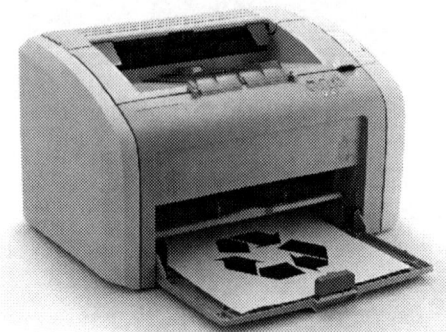

Name:

_____

Worksheet 2.2 (continued)

4

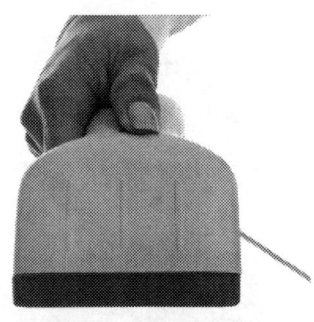

Name:

_____

5

Name:

_____

6

Name:

_____

Worksheet 2.2 (continued)

7

Name:

_____

8

Name:

_____

9

Name:

_____

ICT FOR IGCSE® TEACHER RESOURCE KIT © Oxford University Press 2012

Worksheet 2.2 [continued]

10

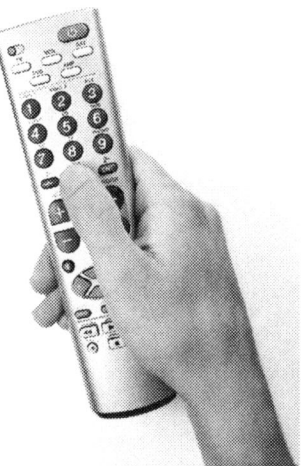

Name:

_____

Topic 2 answers

Questions A

Student book page 20

1 **a** One mark for each correct tick in boxes for the following:

Graphics tablet

Mouse

Microphone

Touch screen

Digital still camera

Web cam

b One mark each for:

Colour laser printer

Speakers

2 **a** One mark for an answer similar to the following:

Used to capture data from the outside world in a form that the computer can process.

b One mark each for two input devices that must be appropriate for a desktop computer such as:

Mouse

Keyboard

Microphone

Touchpad

Touch screen

Scanner

Digital camera

Web cam

c One mark for

Touchpad

3 **a** One mark for keyboard

b One mark for optical mark reader

c One mark for scanner

d One mark for magnetic stripe reader

e One mark for microphone

f One mark for optical mark reader

4 One mark each for two suitable answers such as:

Keyboard

Mouse

Touchpad

Touch screen

5 **a** One mark for bar code reader/laser scanner

b One mark for each point to a maximum of three marks:

Reads the pattern of light and dark lines on the bar code

This is used to represent a number such as the item number

This number is looked up by the computer in a database

Details of the item can be displayed on the screen

c Two appropriate applications (one mark each) such as:

Used to record stock items in a warehouse

Used to hold description, price, number in stock, etc., at the checkout of a supermarket

Questions B

Student book page 24

1 **a** Mouse

b Magnetic stripe reader

c Numeric keypad

d Bar code reader

e Touch screen

2 One mark for each point to a maximum of four marks.

Laser printers are more expensive especially for colour

Inkjet can produce high quality colour images cheaply

Laser printers are much faster

Laser printers are cheaper to run if lots of copies are printed regularly

If you are only printing in black and white then a laser printer would be best

For home use where relatively few copies are printed and you also need to print in colour, then an inkjet printer would be best

Inkjet printers can smudge the ink

Revision questions

Student book page 25

1 **a** One mark for each correct output device.

LCD screen

Laser printer

Speakers

b One mark each for two output devices such as:

Motor

Actuator

Plotter

Multimedia projector

Robot arm

Lathe

c One mark for an input device such as:

Magnetic stripe reader

Optical character reader

ICT FOR IGCSE® TEACHER RESOURCE KIT   © Oxford University Press 2012

Optical mark reader

Bar code reader

Remote control

Tracker ball

Joystick

Scanner

d One mark for one of the following:

Portable hard drive

Flash/pen drive

2 a i One mark for each use to a maximum of two marks:

Making selections

Bring up a menu of items using right click

Issuing a command

Dragging and dropping

Etc.

ii One mark for each use to a maximum of two marks:

Recording live music

Dictating text using voice recognition

Using voicemail

Issuing a command using voice recognition

Recording speech/narration to add to a web site or presentation

iii One mark for each use to a maximum of two marks:

Taking digital still photographs

Taking digital video

Using as a web cam

Using to produce frames for animation

b One mark for the name of each output device and one mark for the use.

Examples include:

Printer (1) to produce a hard copy (1)

Screen (1) to display web pages (1)

Plotter (1) to produce a map or plan on paper (1)

Speakers (1) to listen to music (1)

Etc.

3 One mark for each correct answer (i.e. total of 10 marks).

Application	Most suitable output device
Alerting the user that an error has occurred by making a beep.	Loudspeaker/speaker
Printing a poster in colour.	Inkjet/laser printer
Listening to a radio station using the Internet	Loudspeaker/speaker/headphones
Producing a large plan of a house	Plotter/graph plotter
Producing a hard copy of a spreadsheet	Printer (any type)

Producing a colour picture on paper taken with a digital camera	Inkjet printer/colour laser printer
Producing a series of invoices with several copies that can be sent to different departments	Dot matrix printer
Producing a warning when a bar code is read incorrectly	Loudspeaker/speaker
For listening to messages from a voicemail system	Loudspeaker/speaker
Displaying the results of a quick search on the availability of a holiday	Screen/monitor/VDU

4 a One mark for each point allocated in the following way:

Items/Icons/Menus appear on the screen

You touch the item on the screen to make a selection

b One mark for an advantage such as:

They can be easily used whilst standing up

They are very simple to use as you just touch the item you want

There is no complicated keyboard to use

5 a One mark for: Laser printer

b One mark for: Inkjet printer

c One mark for: Inkjet printer

d One mark for: Inkjet printer

e One mark for: Laser printer

f One mark for: Inkjet printer

Test Yourself

Student book page 26

A input

B keyboard

C mouse

D touchpad

E joysticks

F microphone

G scanner

H optical character recognition

I digital

J stylus

K sensors

L output

M laser

N inkjet

O touch

Examination questions

Student book page 27

1 One mark each for the following items ringed:

Graph plotter

Projector

2 One mark for each correct answer matching:

Scanner – For digitizing an old photograph so it can be put on a website

Touch screen – Used when making selections when buying a train ticket

Chip reader – Reading information on a credit/debit card

Microphone – For recording narration to be used with a presentation

3 One mark for each correct answer.

 a Dot matrix

 b Graph plotters

 c Touch screens

 d Inkjet

4 One mark for each of the following:

Dot matrix printer advantages

Can be used with continuous stationery

Can be used to print multi-part stationery/carbon copies

Cheaper to run compared to inkjet and laser printers

Can print through a payslip cover so that pay details are kept confidential

Dot matrix printer disadvantages

More expensive to buy

Very noisy

Low quality printouts can make the text harder to read

Relatively slow

Laser printer advantages

Very fast output

Relatively quiet compared to inkjet and dot matrix printers

No wet pages that smudge like the inkjet printer

Supplies last longer

Laser printer disadvantages

More expensive running costs than a dot matrix printer

More expensive to buy initially than an inkjet printer

Size as most laser printers are larger than inkjet printers

Advantages of inkjet printers

High quality print makes them ideal for printing photographs

Quieter than a dot matrix printer

Cheaper to purchase initially

Disadvantages of inkjet printers

Inkjet cartridges do not last long

The ink on the paper can smudge

Hard to print a sealed secured payslip

Inkjet cartridges are expensive so this makes them expensive to run

5 A = Trackerball

 B = Scanner

 C = Chip reader

 D = Joystick

6 One mark for each correct answer.

 a A graph plotter.

 b A multimedia projector

 c A pressure sensor

 d A touchpad

 e A microphone

Worksheet 2.1: Can you work out what the word is?

Teacher Resource Kit page 16

1 web cam

2 sensors

3 mouse

4 microphone

5 scanner

6 keyboard

7 joystick

8 stripe

9 interactive

10 graphics

Worksheet 2.2: Can you name the input or output devices shown?

Teacher Resource Kit page 18

1 Mouse

2 Speakers/loudspeakers

3 Printer

4 Bar code reader

5 Digital camera

6 Microphone

7 Web cam

8 Screen/plasma screen

9 Plotter

10 Remote control

ICT FOR IGCSE® TEACHER RESOURCE KIT © Oxford University Press 2012

Storage devices and media

Worksheet 3.1

The differences between the two types of memory ROM and RAM

You have to decide whether each of the following statements refers to ROM or RAM by placing a tick in the relevant columns.

	Statement	ROM	RAM
1	Stands for Read only memory		
2	Stands for Random access memory		
3	Loses its contents when the power is switched off		
4	Contents remain when the power is switched off		
5	Classed as volatile memory		
6	Classed as non-volatile memory		
7	Is read/write		
8	Is read only		
9	The user is able to alter its contents		
10	Used to hold the instructions needed to start the computer up		

Worksheet 3.2

Can you name the storage device/media shown?

Give the name of the storage device/media shown.

1

Name:

_____

2

Name:

_____

3

Name:

_____

ICT FOR IGCSE® TEACHER RESOURCE KIT   © Oxford University Press 2012

Worksheet 3.2 (continued)

4

Name:

_____

5

Name:

_____

Topic 3 answers

Questions A

Student book page 32

1   One mark for each of the following:

Hard drive

CD RW drive

Pen drive

2   a   One mark for Digital Versatile Disk Recordable

b   One mark for Digital Versatile Disk Read Write

3   a   One mark for an answer similar to the following:

A copy of original programs and data kept in case the original data is damaged or lost.

b   So that only a small amount of data would be lost should the original data or programs be damaged or lost.

c   One mark for the name and two marks for two points explaining its suitability.

Portable hard disk

Can be stored in a different place to the original data

Data can be stored on the device at high speed

Revision questions

Student book page 33

1   a   i   One mark for each of the following to a maximum of two marks:

Storing applications programs

Storing the operating system software

Storing user data

ii   One mark for each of the following to a maximum of two marks:

For copying downloaded music so it can be used on a CD player

For distributing programs

To hold music

b   One mark each for two ways such as:

High capacities mean users are not restricted with how much data can be held

Possible to make them very small so the whole piece of equipment can be made small

They are light to make them more portable

2   a   One mark for a difference such as:

Main internal memory is stored in a chip

Backing storage holds a lot more data

Main internal memory offers faster retrieval

b   One mark for an answer similar to the following:

Data currently being processed

Current program instructions

c   One mark for an answer similar to the following:

Data which needs to be stored permanently

Programs which need to be installed

3   One mark for each use and two marks for the explanation.

a   Used for the storage of digital photographs (1) in digital cameras (1) because the cards have a high capacity and are small and light (1).

b   Used for storage of programs (1) as most computers are equipped with CD drives (1) capable of reading the programs so that they can be installed (1).

c   Used for the storage of programs and data (1) because of their very high storage capacity (1) and the high speed at which they read and write data (1).

d   Used for the storage of data (1) and ideal for the transfer of data between computers (1), for example for transferring data between school and home (1).

Test yourself

Student book page 33

A   backups

B   immediately

C   backing

D   programs

E   hard

F   cartridges

G   DVD

Examination questions

Student book page 33

1   One mark each for the following ringed items:

Flash memory card

Magnetic disc

2   One mark each for three reasons:

Pen drives have a higher storage capacity

Pen drives are more portable

They offer faster access to data

They are more robust/CDs are easily scratched

They can be more secure as they can be protected using biometric methods such as fingerprinting

No additional hardware is needed as pen drives simply slot into a USB port

3 A = DVD RAM

B = Pen drive

C = Magnetic tape

D = Magnetic disc

4 One mark each for two of the following:

Portable hard disks have a higher storage capacity

Their transfer rate is higher meaning that less time is spent transferring the files

They are larger in size which means they are less likely to be lost or stolen

Worksheet 3.1: The differences between the two types of memory ROM and RAM

Teacher Resource Kit page 25

	Statement	ROM	RAM
1	Stands for Read only memory	√	
2	Stands for Random access memory		√
3	Loses its contents when the power is switched off		√
4	Contents remain when the power is switched off	√	
5	Classed as volatile memory		√
6	Classed as non-volatile memory	√	
7	Is read/write		√
8	Is read only	√	
9	The user is able to alter its contents		√
10	Used to hold the instructions needed to start the computer up	√	

Worksheet 3.2: Can you name the storage device/media shown?

Teacher Resource Kit page 26

1 Magnetic hard drive/hard drive

2 CD RW

3 Memory stick/pen drive/USB drive/flash memory

4 Memory card

5 Memory chips/RAM or ROM/main memory

4 Computer networks

Worksheet 4.1

Can you work out what the word is?

Here are some words or phrases which have been jumbled up. The words are
connected with keeping data safe and secure. Can you work out what they are?
There is a clue to help you.

1 Prince tony

Hint: Method of keeping data private.

Answer: _____

2 Sack her

Hint: People who gain illegal access to a computer.

Answer: _____

3 Buck pa

Hint: You must remember to take this.

Answer:_____ _____ _____ _____

4 Cress lamb

Hint: What encryption does to the data.

Answer: _____

5 Grin

Hint: Type of network topology.

Answer: _____

6 Sub

Hint: Type of network topology.

Answer: _____

ICT FOR IGCSE® TEACHER RESOURCE KIT   © Oxford University Press 2012

Worksheet 4.1 (continued)

7 Enter tin

Hint: The largest network.

Answer: _____

8 Near tint

Hint: A network used inside an organization.

Answer: _____

9 True or

Hint: Device for joining networks.

Answer: _____

10 Air do

Hint: Type of signal used to send information.

Answer: _____

Topic 4 answers

Questions A

Student book page 37

1 One mark for each benefit to a maximum of two marks.

You can send and receive email from anyone on the LAN

You can share the same data files

Software can be updated centrally

Hardware devices such as printers and scanners can be shared

2 One mark for each difference to a maximum of two marks.

LAN (local area network)	WAN (wide area network)
Confined to a small area	Cover a wide geographical area (e.g. between cities, countries and even continents).
Usually located in a single building	In lots of different buildings and cities, countries, etc.
Uses cable, wireless, infra-red and microwave links which are usually owned by the organization	Uses more expensive telecommunication links that are supplied by telecommunication companies (e.g. satellite links)
Cheaper to build as equipment is owned by the organization	Expensive to build as sophisticated communication systems are used
Slower speed connections	High speed connections
Cheaper to run as less expertise is needed	Expensive to run as highly qualified and expensive staff are needed to keep network running

3 One mark each for two advantages and two disadvantages.

Advantages

➤ You can share hardware – you share printers, scanners and the equipment such as modems and routers used to provide an Internet connection.

➤ Software can be installed in one place – you do not need to install software on each computer. This makes it faster to install and easier to maintain. If the software needs to be upgraded, then this is much easier if only one copy is used.

➤ Work can be backed up centrally by the network manager, which means users do not have to back up their own work. The network manager will make sure that the work is backed up.

➤ Passwords make sure that other people cannot access your work unless you want them to.

➤ Speed – it is very quick to copy and transfer files.

➤ Cost – network versions of software can be bought and these are much cheaper than buying a copy for each stand-alone computer.

➤ Email facilities – any user of the network will be able to communicate using electronic mail. This will be much more efficient compared to paper-based documents such as memos, etc.

➤ Access to a central store of data – users will have access to centrally stored data.

Disadvantages

➤ A network manager will need to be employed – this can be quite expensive.

➤ Security problems – a virus could get onto the system and cause problems, or hackers may gain access to the data on the network.

➤ Breakdown problems – if the network breaks down, users will not have access to the important information held.

➤ Expensive – a server and cables and/or other communication devices will be needed. The installation costs of a network are also high.

4 a Two marks for:

The devices in a network may be arranged in different way and each way is called a topology. It is the way a network is connected either by wires or wirelessly.

b One mark for each of two names:

Ring

Bus

Tree

5 a One mark for each name in a suitable pair of devices such as:

Keyboard and computer

Mouse and computer

Mobile phone and computer

Camera and computer

Computer and printer

Etc.

b One mark for an advantage such as:

No direct connection is needed so it is easier

No need to hunt for a cable to make the connection

c One mark for a disadvantage such as:

Bluetooth only has a short range which limits its use

There is a danger of hackers accessing the system

6 One mark for each advantage to a maximum of two marks:

No wires to sink/conceal

Can work anywhere in the office or even close to the office outside

Easier to keep the offices clean

Fewer trailing wires to trip over

7 a One mark for a reason such as:

Lower installation costs as there are no network wires to buy and install

Can work anywhere in the building

b One mark for: So that several/many computers can share a single connection to the Internet.

ICT FOR IGCSE® TEACHER RESOURCE KIT © Oxford University Press 2012

8 One mark for: They may be worried that hackers may gain access to the network.

Questions B

Student book page 39

1 One mark for each of two differences such as:

An intranet is a private network used with an organization that makes use of Internet technology used for sharing internal information.

The Internet is a huge network of networks which anyone can access.

The information on an intranet is confined to information related to a particular company or organization.

The information on the Internet is about every subject imaginable.

Intranet access is restricted to certain groups of people such as the staff working in an organization.

2 a One mark for Internet service provider

b One mark each for two services such as:

Storage on their server, where you can store your web site

Email facilities

Instant messages where you can send short messages to your friends when they are online

Access to online shopping

Access to news, sport, weather, financial pages, etc.

3 One mark for each point to a maximum of two marks.

Web browser software is a program (1) that allows web pages stored on the Internet to be viewed (1). Web browsers read the instructions on how to display the items on a webpage (1) which are written in a form called HTML (Hypertext Markup Language)(1).

Questions C

Student book page 43

1 One mark for router/wireless router.

2 a Two advantages (one mark each) such as:

Ability to send and receive emails

Able to watch TV or listen to radio programmes

Access to huge amounts of information

Can use banking facilities without leaving your home

Can shop online and get goods delivered to your home

Etc.

b Two disadvantages (one mark each) such as:

Danger of introducing viruses

Danger of hackers accessing your personal data

Misinformation – as some sites give you incorrect details

Inappropriate content

Etc.

3 a One mark for each point to a maximum of two marks.

ICT system that allows virtual face-to-face meetings (1) to be conducted without the participants being in the same room or even the same geographical area (1).

b One mark each for two benefits such as:

Less stress as employees do not have to experience delays at airports, accidents, road works, etc.

Improved family life, as less time spent away from home staying in hotels.

They do not have to put in long working hours travelling to and from meetings.

Saves money as business does not have to spend money on travelling expenses, hotel rooms, meals, etc.

Improved productivity of employees, as they are not wasting time travelling.

Meetings can be called at very short notice without too much planning.

Greener/more environmentally friendly as there are fewer people flying to meetings. This cuts down on carbon dioxide emissions.

Roads will not be clogged up with traffic and this will cause less stress and reduce pollution.

4 Two marks for an answer such as:

A hub contains multiple ports (i.e. connection points)

A switch is a device that is able to inspect packets of data so that they are forwarded appropriately to the correct computer

Switches are more intelligent than hubs

A switch reduces the amount of data on a network

5 One mark for each point to a maximum of two marks.

They can use then to block offensive web content such as pornography.

They can be used to protect the anonymity of the network to protect against hackers.

Revision questions

Student book page 43

1 a i Local area network

ii Wide area network

b Two differences for two marks as outlined in this table.

LAN (local area network)	WAN (wide area network)
Confined to a small area	Cover a wide geographical area (e.g. between cities, countries and even continents)
Usually located in a single building	In lots of different buildings and cities, countries, etc.

Uses cable, wireless, infra-red and microwave links which are usually owned by the organization	Uses more expensive telecommunication links that are supplied by telecommunication companies (e.g. satellite links)
Cheaper to build as equipment is owned by the organization	Expensive to build as sophisticated communication systems are used
Slower speed connections	High speed connections
Cheaper to run as less expertise is needed	Expensive to run as highly qualified and expensive staff are needed to keep network running

c One mark for each advantage to a maximum of three marks.

You can share hardware – you share printers, scanners and the equipment such as modems and routers used to provide an Internet connection.

Software can be installed in one place – you do not need to install software on each computer. This makes it faster to install and easier to maintain. If the software needs to be upgraded, then this is much easier if only one copy is used.

Work can be backed up centrally by the network manager, which means users do not have to back up their own work. The network manager will make sure that the work is backed up.

Passwords make sure that other people cannot access your work unless you want them to.

Speed – it is very quick to copy and transfer files.

Cost – network versions of software can be bought and these are much cheaper than buying a copy for each stand-alone computer.

Email facilities – any user of the network will be able to communicate using electronic mail. This will be much more efficient compared to paper-based documents such as memos, etc.

Access to a central store of data – users will have access to centrally stored data.

Backups are taken centrally – a network manager is responsible for taking regular backups. Users of stand-alone computers may forget to take backups.

d One mark for 'Encrypt/scramble the data'.

2 a One mark for Credit/debit card.

b One mark for each point to a maximum of two marks.

Their details may be hacked into

The details can then be used to commit fraud

c One mark each for two points:

Details are encrypted (1) which means that if they are hacked into they cannot be understood (1).

3 a One mark each for two points similar to the following:

Tells the network who is using the computer

Details can be added to the transaction log

Can tell who has accessed and altered files

b One mark each for two points similar to the following:

Ensure that the person who is using the user-ID is the correct person

Used to prevent unauthorized access

Used to prevent hackers accessing the network

c One mark each for two points similar to the following:

Scrambles the data

Only the correct recipient can view the data

Stored or passed through a network

So that if intercepted or stolen it cannot be understood

4 One mark each for an advantage/disadvantage up to a maximum of four marks.

Advantages

Provided you have a wireless signal anywhere in the building

Fewer/no trailing wires to trip over

It is easier to keep a working area clean if there are not as many wires in the way

No network wires so no cost associated with sinking them

Disadvantages

The danger of hackers reading messages

There are areas where you cannot get a wireless network

There is some evidence that there may be a danger to your health

Limited signal range

5 a One mark each for two advantages:

Less stress as employees do not have to experience delays at airports, accidents, road works, etc.

Improved family life, as less time spent away from home staying in hotels.

They do not have to put in long working hours travelling to and from meetings.

Saves money as business does not have to spend money on travelling expenses, hotel rooms, meals, etc.

Improved productivity of employees, as they are not wasting time travelling.

Meetings can be called at very short notice without too much planning.

Greener as there are fewer people flying to meetings. This cuts down on carbon dioxide emissions.

Roads will not be clogged up with traffic and this will cause less stress and reduce pollution.

b One mark each for two disadvantages:

The cost of the equipment, as specialist videoconferencing equipment is expensive.

Poor image and sound quality.

People can feel very self-conscious when using videoconferencing and may fail to come across well.

Although documents and diagrams in digital form can be passed around, an actual product or component cannot be passed around.

Lack of face-to-face contact may mean a discussion may not be as effective.

If the delegates are in distant locations, there can be a time lag, which can be distracting.

Test yourself

Student book page 43

A   wireless

B   encrypted

C   Bluetooth

D   synchronize

E   Local

F   Wide

G   Internet

H   hackers

I   Videoconferencing

J   Web browser

Examination questions

Student book page 44

1 One mark for each correct answer.

a a hub

b an intranet

c a proxy server

d a WLAN

2 One mark for each correct answer.

A router – to enable data to be transferred from one network to another

A browser – to enable web pages to be viewed on the World Wide Web

Email – so that messages can be sent to people who are external to the home network

An ISP – in order to be able to access the Internet/In order to be able to send emails to users outside the home network

3 a One mark for network card.

b One mark for each of the following to a maximum of two marks:

Reduced cabling costs

Reduced installation costs because there are fewer cables to lay

Very easy to connect extra devices to the network

Computers can connect to the network anywhere in the building provided there is a signal

c One mark for each of the following to a maximum of two marks:

Can only be used to transfer data when the distances are small

The rate of data transfer is very slow compared to a wired network

Greater risk of the interception of the data from hackers

Only supports a limited number of devices in a network

d One mark for the reason and one mark for a further detail x 3.

They may be worried that unauthorized users could get onto the network (1) and compromise the security of the network by viewing/altering/deleting data (1).

Data such as bank account details could be stolen by hackers (1) and used to commit fraud (1).

Spyware could be used (1) to log keystrokes so that passwords could be obtained (1).

There could be accidental loss of data (1) due to inexperienced operators, which could result in not being paid (1).

Without proper access controls, employees could access the payroll files (1) and learn how much each employee earned (1).

A virus could be introduced onto the network (1) which could result in the damage or deletion of important payroll files (1).

e One mark each for three of the following:

Use biometrics (e.g., retinal scanning, fingerprinting) for access control

Encrypt data

Use a system of usernames and passwords

Install anti-virus software

Introduce a firewall

Use physical security such as locks on doors; security guards

Install anti-spyware

Use a proxy server

Don't allow the internal network to connect to the Internet

4 One mark each for any five from the following:

LAN stands for local area network

WAN stands for wide area network

LAN is used in a limited geographical area/ in one building or on one site

WAN is used over a wide geographical area spanning towns/countries

It is more difficult to share peripherals (e.g. scanners and printers) using a WAN

WANs consist of many LANs linked together

WANs usually use expensive telecommunications equipment which is hired from telecommunications companies

Worksheet 4.1: Can you work out what the word is?

Teacher Resource Kit page 30

1 Encryption
2 Hackers
3 Backup
4 Scrambles
5 Ring
6 Bus
7 Internet
8 Intranet
9 Router
10 Radio

Data types

5

Can you work out what the word is?

Here are some words or phrases which have been jumbled up. The words are connected with database software. Can you work out what they are? There is a clue to help you.

1 Ale boon

Hint: Data type where there are two alternatives.

Answer: _____

2 Cod err

Hint: Part of a file.

Answer: _____

3 Filed

Hint: Part of a file.

Answer: _____

4 Bleat

Hint: Something you organize data in.

Answer: _____

Topic 5 answers

Questions A

Student book page 45

1 One mark for each correct answer.

Name of field	Example data	Data type
Title	(Mr, Mrs, Ms, Dr, etc.)	Alphanumeric/text
Phone number	0798273232	Alphanumeric/text
Sex	M or F	Logical/Boolean
Country	Botswana	Alphanumeric/text
Date of birth	01/10/03	Date
Years at address	4	Numeric

2 One mark for each correct answer.

Items of data	Tick if data type is logical/Boolean
Driving licence (yes or no)	√
Sex (M or F)	√
Size (S, M, L, XL, XXL)	
Airport code	
Car registration number	
Date of purchase	
Car type (manual or automatic)	√
Fuel type (diesel or petrol)	√

Questions B

Student book page 48

1 a One mark each for two from: Reg-number, Make, Model or Year.

b One mark for Reg-number

c One mark for an explanation such as:

It is the only field which is unique

No two registration numbers are the same

d One mark for 7

2 a One mark for each of three correct fields:

  i Alphanumeric

  ii Alphanumeric

  iii Boolean/Logical

b Three fields (one mark each) such as:

Form teacher

Form

Date of entry

Exam results

Pupil email address

Pupil mobile number

Name of parent/guardian

Parent/guardian work telephone number

Medical problems

Medication taken

c One mark for the name of the field and one mark for an explanation.

UniquePupilNumber – as no two pupils can have the same number, so it is used to identify pupils who could have the same names.

d One mark each for two errors such as:

Transcription errors – where data copied from forms is misread

Transposition errors – where digits are incorrectly reversed when being typed into the database

e One mark for each method that is applicable to the answer in part d.

Verification where after the data is keyed in it is carefully checked against the original document used to supply the information such as an application form

Validation checks such as a check digit added to the unique pupil number which checks that all the other numbers in the pupil number have been input correctly

3 a One mark for one of the following:

A database consisting of a single table of data

A list of data created using spreadsheet software

b One mark for:

A database where the data is held in two or more tables with relationships forming links between the tables.

c One mark for a statement of the application and one mark for a reason why the application is suitable. An example answer is as follows:

For a simple list of contact details (1), so that they can be searched easily and used as the contact details for a mail merge (1).

4 a One mark for each difference to a maximum of two marks.

Flat file has all the data in a single table (1) whereas a relational database contains the data in two or more tables (1).

There are no relationships in a flat-file database because there is only one table (1) whereas in a relational database there are relationships between the tables (1).

b One mark for each of three points similar to the following:

Relational database

Three tables are needed: Customer, Dresses and Rentals

Would avoid duplicated data/redundancy

Less data would need to be input

It would be easier to keep the data up-to-date

The data could be extracted more flexibly

ICT FOR IGCSE® TEACHER RESOURCE KIT   © Oxford University Press 2012

Test yourself

Student book page 50

- A real
- B alphanumeric
- C Boolean
- D key field
- E record
- F fields
- G relational
- H table
- I links
- J foreign
- K redundancy
- L digital
- M analogue to digital
- N digital, digital to analogue

Revision questions

Student book page 51

1 a One mark for each sensible field name up to a maximum of four marks such as:

Surname

Initial

Address/First line address

Postcode

Telephone number

b i One mark for any answer similar to the following:

Key field has to be unique

Surname is not unique as there are two people with the same surname

ii One mark for one of the following:
Employee ID

Employee No.

Etc.

2 a One mark for each of the following key fields:

Customer number and Item code

b One mark for Delivery

c One mark each for two sensible fields such as:

Date of order, Description of item, Qty ordered, VAT, etc.

d One mark for 4.

3 a One mark for:

Sensors read analogue data that is continuously changing (1) whereas most computers can only process data in digital form (1).

b One mark for: Analogue to digital converter (ADC).

Examination questions

Student book page 52

1 a One mark for each of three sensors:

Moisture

Humidity

Temperature

Light

b One mark for each of two points such as:

Sensors usually supply data in analogue form

Computers can only process and store data in digital form so conversion from analogue to digital is needed

2 a 4

b 5

c Relational database

d Two marks for two reasons such as:

Easier to maintain referential integrity/Data does not have to be typed twice

It is faster to enter new data

So fewer errors are likely

So less memory/storage capacity is needed

So it is easier to edit data

e Code

f Book borrowed

g Cost

h Date

3 a One mark each for three of the following:

Pressure

Temperature

Moisture

Humidity

Motion

Light

b Two marks allocated as follows:

Sensors produce analogue data (1) but computers can only read and process digital data (1).

c One mark for analogue to digital converter.

Worksheet 5.1: Can you work out what the word is?

Teacher Resource Kit page 37

1 Boolean

2 Record

3 Field

4 Table

6 The effects of using ICT

Worksheet 6.1

Can you work out what the word is?

Here are some words or phrases which have been jumbled up. The words are connected with health issues from using ICT. Can you work out what they are? There is a clue to help you.

1 A retentive injury trip is

Hint: RSI

Answer: _____

2 Erase tiny

Hint: You get this by looking at the screen for long periods.

Answer: _____

3 A cab heck

Hint: Incorrect posture when sitting gives you this.

Answer: _____

4 Chase head

Hint: Eye strain can give you these.

Answer: _____

5 Jab saluted

Hint: All chairs used with computers should be this.

Answer: _____

6 Cut demon

Hint: A _____ holder.

Answer: _____

ICT FOR IGCSE® TEACHER RESOURCE KIT   © Oxford University Press 2012

Worksheet 6.1 (continued)

7 **Large**

Hint: Use blinds on windows to prevent this on the screen.

Answer: _____

8 **Crime goons**

Hint: The science of making things used by humans easier to use.

Answer: _____

9 **Pouters**

Hint: Incorrect _____ can cause back ache.

Answer: _____

10 **Burr led**

Hint: Stress and headaches can give rise to this problem with vision.

Answer: _____

Worksheet 6.2

The way ICT has changed or even eliminated some jobs

Some jobs have been eliminated by ICT developments; others have been created, whilst other jobs have been changed. There are some jobs that have not been affected at all by ICT developments.

Here are some jobs. For each job state with a reason whether the job has been **eliminated**, **created**, **changed** or **unaffected** by ICT developments.

a Call centre work _____

b Web site designer _____

c Selling mobile telephones _____

d Filing clerk _____

e Typewriter repair person _____

f Secretary _____

g Painter and decorator _____

h Doctor _____

i Teacher _____

j Computer programmer _____

k Writer _____

ICT FOR IGCSE® TEACHER RESOURCE KIT © Oxford University Press 2012

Worksheet 6.3

Social networking and web log terms – how well up on them are you?

There has been a huge increase in the use of social networking and web log sites over the last few years. There are a number of terms which are associated with social networking and web logs. Many of these terms are now so popular you can find them in the latest dictionaries. How many do you know? If you are unsure, have a guess – you will probably be right.

Write your definition or meaning in the space provided.

1 Social networking

Meaning: _____

_____

_____

2 Web logs (blogs)

Meaning: _____

_____

_____

3 Blogger

Meaning: _____

_____

_____

4 Tweet

Meaning: _____

_____

_____

5 Defriend

Meaning: _____

_____

_____

Worksheet 6.3 (continued)

6 **Social notworking**

   Meaning: _____

   _____

   _____

7 **Anti-social networking site**

   Meaning: _____

   _____

   _____

8 **Twitter**

   Meaning: _____

   _____

   _____

ICT FOR IGCSE® TEACHER RESOURCE KIT   © Oxford University Press 2012

Worksheet 6.4

Has the use of ICT had a positive or negative impact?

Some ICT developments have had positive effects on our lives while others have produced negative effects. Here are some things/situations and you have to decide whether they are positive or negative by completing the boxes in the following table.

Comments about ICT	Positive or negative?
It is very hard to keep your personal life private.	
New problems have been created such as cyberbullying.	
People are worried about having their identity stolen.	
Your personal life is no longer your own.	
Communication, wherever you are, is easier.	
Widens the gap between the haves and the have-nots.	
Creates a new group of ICT-related crimes.	
There are health problems associated with working with ICT equipment.	
Allows disabled people to work.	
Some employees are able to work from home.	
Using the Internet to shop means that you have a much greater choice of products and services to choose from.	
Using ICT can be very stressful.	
Mobile phones allow communication between people on the move (taxi drivers, reps, etc.).	
More realistic computer games are available that are more fun.	
Paying for goods is much faster using ICT.	
Mobile phones are useful in an emergency.	
You can use the Internet for research and this saves a trip to the library.	

Activity 6.1

The trouble caused by viruses

Viruses cause computer users all sorts of problems and you may have had problems with them yourself. Viruses can cause organizations huge amounts of problems which cost a lot of money to put right.

For this activity you have to use the Internet to find some examples of the problems caused by virus attacks.

Collect your research material and then produce a word-processed document that outlines four cases where viruses have caused problems.

Activity 6.2

Keeping viruses out

There are many ways you can keep viruses out of an ICT system.

You have to produce a poster for the computer room outlining what steps a user can take to keep viruses out of their system.

Activity 6.3

Creating an interactive presentation on health and safety issues at work

Every new employee of an organization gets an induction pack when they start work at the organization. Part of this induction pack consists of some health and safety training on the safe use of ICT equipment.

You have been asked to produce a presentation using presentation software.

There are a number of requirements of the system and these are:

▸▸ The system is intended to be used by one employee at a time sitting at a computer.

▸▸ The system must be easy to use as they will be working on their own.

▸▸ It should be possible for the user to decide what they want to do next, so you will need some form of navigation around the system.

▸▸ The presentation should be fun to use.

▸▸ The target audience will be employees so your presentation must meet their needs.

▸▸ Appropriate images should be included.

You could try including some health and safety video if you can find a source.

Activity 6.4

Researching equipment that will reduce the risk of potential health hazards when working with ICT

There are many pieces of equipment that can be used to reduce the risk of potential health hazards when working with ICT. In this activity you have to research them.

For each piece of equipment you need to obtain an image and write a few sentences about its purpose and what potential health hazard it avoids.

Activity 6.5

What are these for?

Here are some health and safety products which can be used when staff use computers to help prevent certain health problems. Can you work out what each of them is for? Write a short sentence to explain.

1

2

3

4

ICT FOR IGCSE® TEACHER RESOURCE KIT   © Oxford University Press 2012

Activity 6.5 (continued)

5

6

7

Topic 6 answers

Questions A

Student book page 55

1 **a** Two marks allocated in the following way:

Program that copies itself automatically (1) and causes damage to data or causes the computer to run slowly (1)

b Two marks allocated in the following way:

Illegally accessing a computer system (1)

With a view to viewing the data (1)

With a view to stealing the identity of a person/company (1)

2 **a** One mark for anti-virus software.

b One mark for each of two actions such as:

Don't open file attachments unless you know who they are from

Don't download files from unknown sources

3 **a** One mark for:

To authenticate the user; to prove to the system that the user who supplied the username is the authorized user

b One mark for:

If the password becomes known by someone else, then it could only be used for a short period before it is changed

Questions B

Student book page 57

1 **a** Two jobs (one mark each) such as:

Filing clerk

Typist

Welder

Paint sprayer in a car factory

Packers

Stock takers

Shop assistants

Post clerk

b Any two jobs that have an obvious ICT connection such as:

Managers

Shop checkout staff

Doctor

Etc.

c One job for one mark such as:

Call centre staff

Telephone help line staff

Online bank advisor

Airline booking clerk

Telephone marketing staff

2 **a** Three jobs (one mark each) such as:

Network managers

Web site designers

Development staff/programmers/systems analysts

Computer sales staff

ICT repair staff/engineers

b One mark each for two points such as:

New ICT systems are being introduced all the time

The technology is constantly changing

New hardware and software are used

Staff need to know how to work with these new systems

Questions C

Student book page 62

1 **a** One mark for each of three health problems (no mark for a one-word answer) such as:

Back ache caused by incorrect posture when sitting in a chair

Repetitive strain injury (RSI) caused by typing at high speed

Eye strain caused by focusing on the screen for too long

b One mark for each of six points such as:

Use an adjustable chair (NB in work this may be a legal requirement but you need to ensure that the chair you use at home is adjustable)

Always check the adjustment of the chair to make sure it is suitable for your height – use a foot support (called a footrest) if necessary

Sit up straight on the chair with your feet flat on the floor

Make sure the screen is lined up and tilted at an appropriate angle

Use appropriate lighting and blinds to avoid glare, which can cause headaches

Take regular breaks to give your eyes a rest

Have regular eye-tests (NB if you use a screen in your work, then your employer may be required by law to pay for regular eye-tests and glasses if they are needed)

Ensure you are not sitting too near the screen to avoid the possible risks of radiation

2 **a** One mark for: Repetitive strain injury.

b One mark for one of the following:

Aches and pains in hands

Aches and pains in wrists

Aches and pains in arms

c One mark each for two of the following precautions:

Adjust the chair to the correct seating position for you

Make sure there is enough space to work comfortably

Use a document holder

Use a wrist rest

Keep wrists straight when keying in

Position the mouse so that it can be used keeping the wrist straight

Learn how to type properly – two-finger typing has been found to be much worse for RSI

3 One mark for each correct answer.

TRUE

FALSE

TRUE

TRUE

FALSE

4 a One mark for:

Unwanted email

Unsolicited email used to advertise goods or services

b One mark for the name and one mark for a brief description of its purpose.

Spam filter

Removes email identified as spam into a folder so it can be deleted

5 a Two marks for two points similar to the following:

Emails sent pretending they are from a bank, credit card company, etc.

They ask you to supply banking or credit card details

b Two marks for two points similar to the following:

If you supply these then the details will be used fraudulently

They can be used to steal your identity

Someone could buy goods and services using your credit/debit card details

Test yourself

Student book page 62

A firewall

B anti-virus

C files

D download

E RSI

F headaches

G back ache

H blinds

I eye tests

J hacking

K phishing

l teleworking

M spam

N pharming

O blogs

P wikis

Revision questions

Student book page 63

1 a One mark for: Repetitive strain injury.

b One mark for each point to a maximum of two marks:

Caused by typing for long periods (1) or using a mouse over a long period of time (1)

Caused by working in cramped conditions (1)

Caused by repeatedly moving head a certain way to read a document and look at the screen (1)

c One mark for one of the following:

Adjust your chair to the correct seating position for you

Make sure there is enough space to work comfortably

Use a document holder

Use an ergonomic keyboard/mouse

Use a wrist rest

Keep your wrists straight when keying in

Position the mouse so that it can be used keeping the wrist straight

Learn how to type properly – two-finger typing has been found to be much worse for RSI

2 One mark each for:

Back ache

Headaches

Repetitive strain injury (RSI)

Eye strain

3 a One mark for each of two health problems (not eye strain or RSI) such as:

Back ache

Neck ache

Headaches

b One mark each for two methods of prevention.

Back ache – use an adjustable chair and make sure you adjust it to suit your height – you can use a foot rest if there is one

Neck ache – ensure the screen is positioned in front of the user/ensure a copyholder is used

Headaches – make sure that fluorescent tubes are used with diffusers on them to spread out the light

4 One mark for three of the following such as:

Computer-controlled production lines

Robots are used to assemble products

For example, assemble cars, spray paint, etc.

There are fewer less-skilled staff and more skilled staff

5 One mark for each correctly placed tick.

	Tick three boxes only
Homeworking/teleworking is more popular	√
Employees are more likely to work more flexibly	√
It has brought about a huge rise in employment especially among factory workers	
Training and re-training are needed regularly	√
Workers are generally less skilled than they were	

Examination questions

Student book page 64

1 One mark for each answer similar to the following:

a Pharming – installing malicious code in a person's computer which directs them to a fake site which looks like a banking site and then get them to reveal personal details

b Phishing – Using fake emails pretending to be from the target's bank to get them to reveal banking/personal details

2 One mark for an explanation of spam similar to the following:

Spam – unwanted/unasked for email/Junk email

One mark for an example such as:

It wastes time having to read and delete it

It takes up storage space before deletion

3 a One mark for each of two health issues such as:

Headaches caused by prolonged computer use

RSI through typing for prolonged periods

Back problems caused by bad posture

One mark for each of two safety issues such as:

Trailing wires in a computer room

Too many plugs in an electric socket

Drinking water while using a computer

4 a One mark for one answer similar to the following:

An online diary of events

An online journal about a person/topic

b One mark for one answer similar to the following:

Virtual communities of people who communicate with each other about a subject or just to make friends using the Internet and a special website

A website that allows members to communicate with each other using instant messaging, email, a type of blog and even voice or videoconferencing

c One mark for one answer similar to the following:

A web page that can be viewed and modified by anyone who has a web browser

A website such as an online encyclopaedia whose content can be added to and edited by users

Worksheet 6.1: Health issues

Teacher Resource Kit page 40

1 Repetitive strain injury

2 Eye strain

3 Back ache

4 Headaches

5 Adjustable

6 Document

7 Glare

8 Ergonomics

9 Posture

10 Blurred

Worksheet 6.2: The way ICT has changed or even eliminated some jobs

Teacher Resource Kit page 42

a Created

b Created

c Created

d Eliminated

e Eliminated

f Changed

g Unaffected

h Changed

i Changed

j Created

k Changed

Worksheet 6.3: Social networking and web log terms – how well up on them are you?

Teacher Resource Kit page 43

1 Social networking

A web site that is used to communicate with friends, family and to make new friends and contacts.

2 Web logs (blogs)

Web sites providing commentary, personal thoughts or news on a particular subject. They are written in chronological order and can include text, images and links to other blogs and web sites.

3 Blogger

A person who posts their comments to a blog.

4 Tweet

A post on the social networking site Twitter.

5 Defriend

Remove a person from your list of friends on a social networking site.

6 Social notworking

Referring to the process of wasting time on social networking sites when you are supposed to be working.

7 Anti-social networking site

A social networking site where you post details of people and things you do not like.

8 Twitter

A simple social networking site which simply asks 'what are you doing now' and you can reply using your computer or mobile phone.

Worksheet 6.4: Has the use of ICT had a positive or negative impact?

Teacher Resource Kit page 45

Comments about ICT	Positive or negative?
It is very hard to keep your personal life private.	Negative
New problems have been created such as cyberbullying.	Negative
People are worried about having their identity stolen.	Negative
Your personal life is no longer your own.	Negative
Communication, wherever you are, is easier.	Positive
Widens the gap between the haves and the have-nots.	Negative
Creates a new group of ICT-related crimes.	Negative

There are health problems associated with working with ICT equipment.	Negative
Allows disabled people to work.	Positive
Some employees are able to work from home.	Positive
Using the Internet to shop means that you have a much greater choice of products and services to choose from.	Positive
Using ICT can be very stressful.	Negative
Mobile phones allow communication between people on the move (taxi drivers, reps, etc.).	Positive
More realistic computer games are available that are more fun.	Positive
Paying for goods is much faster using ICT.	Positive
Mobile phones are useful in an emergency.	Positive
You can use the Internet for research and this saves a trip to the library.	Positive

Activity 6.5: What are these for?

Teacher Resource Kit page 50

1 Mouse mat with a wrist rest filled with gel so that a user is less likely to suffer with RSI.

2 An adjustable arm rest with a mouse mat – used to reduce the likelihood of RSI occurring when using a mouse.

3 A wrist rest to be placed at the front of the keyboard. Provides a cushion for when a user is typing at high speed – it reduces the likelihood of RSI.

4 A foot rest to help a user (particularly a short user) adopt the correct posture when working at a computer.

5 An antiglare or anti-radiation filter. Used to cut down glare which could cause eye strain or headaches. Also could reduce the risk of radiation from the screen – although this is very debateable.

6 An ergonomic mouse which could reduce the likelihood of RSI.

7 A foot controlled mouse – may reduce RSI.

7 The ways in which ICT is used

Worksheet 7.1

Producing a spreadsheet model to simulate depreciation

When you drive a new car out of the showroom it will go down in price. If you tried to sell it back to a garage or privately, you will get less than you paid for it. As you use the car and it gets older, its value goes down. This is called depreciation.

Cars depreciate at different rates depending on the make and model. BMW and Mercedes depreciate less than Fords or Vauxhalls, although they generally cost more to buy in the first place.

In this activity we will try to produce a model for the depreciation for two different new cars over a four-year period:

Car A has a depreciation of 40% per year whilst car B has a depreciation of only 25% per year.

The costs of each car when new are: Car A £13000   Car B £18500

Follow these steps to set up the model.

1   Load the spreadsheet software until you see the blank grid. Now type in the data exactly in the positions shown here:

	A	B	C	D	E	F	G	H
1	A model showing car depreciation							
2				Year 1	Year 2	Year 3	Year 4	
3	Car A	£13,000						
4	Car B	£18,500						
5								
6								

2   In cell D3 type in the formula =0.6*b3

This will calculate 60% of the original price (i.e. 100% – 40%= 60% depreciation which can be written 60/100 or 0.6)

Check that it now looks like this:

	A	B	C	D	E	F	G	H
1	A model showing car depreciation							
2				Year 1	Year 2	Year 3	Year 4	
3	Car A	£13,000		£7,800.0				
4	Car B	£18,500						
5								
6								

3   In cell E3 type in the formula =0.6*d3

This works out 60% of the price after year 1.

In cell F3 type in the formula =0.6*e3

In cell G3 type in the formula = 0.6*f3

ICT FOR IGCSE® TEACHER RESOURCE KIT   © Oxford University Press 2012

Worksheet 7.1 (continued)

Check that the spreadsheet now looks like this:

	A	B	C	D	E	F	G	H
1	A model showing car depreciation							
2				Year 1	Year 2	Year 3	Year 4	
3	Car A	£13,000		£7,800.0	£4,680.0	£2,808.0	£1,684.80	
4	Car B	£18,500						
5								

4 For Car B, the depreciation is 25%. This means that the car is worth 100% – 25% = 75% of its price the previous year.

You have to construct the formulae in a similar way to step 3 using the figure 0.75 to fill in the amounts for Year 1, Year 2, etc.

Your spreadsheet will now look like this:

	A	B	C	D	E	F	G	H
1	A model showing car depreciation							
2				Year 1	Year 2	Year 3	Year 4	
3	Car A	£13,000		£7,800.0	£4,680.0	£2,808.0	£1,684.80	
4	Car B	£18,500		£13,875.00	£10,406.25	£7,804.69	£5,853.52	

5 We can now work out how much the cars have depreciated in total over the four years. In cell H4 put the heading 'Depreciation' (NB you will need to widen the column to fit in the text).

To work out the total depreciation for Car A we subtract the figure in cell G3 from the figure in cell B3. Put the formula =b3–g3 in cell H3.

Put a similar formula =b4–g4 in cell H4.

The final model will look like this:

	A	B	C	D	E	F	G	H
1	A model showing car depreciation							
2				Year 1	Year 2	Year 3	Year 4	Depreciation
3	Car A	£13,000		£7,800.0	£4,680.0	£2,808.0	£1,684.80	£11,315.20
4	Car B	£18,500		£13,875.00	£10,406.25	£7,804.69	£5,853.52	£12,646.48
5								
6								

6 We can now alter the prices and see what happens to the depreciation. Suppose both cars cost exactly the same price but still had the same rates of depreciation. What would happen if they both cost £15,000? Put the value £15,000 into cells B3 and B4.

The model now looks like this:

	A	B	C	D	E	F	G	H
1	A model showing car depreciation							
2				Year 1	Year 2	Year 3	Year 4	Depreciation
3	Car A	£15,000		£9,000.0	£5,400.0	£3,240.0	£1,944.00	£13,056.00
4	Car B	£15,000		£11,250.00	£8,437.50	£6,328.13	£4,746.09	£10,253.91
5								

Worksheet 7.2

Making the model more useful

This car depreciation model is fairly simple. We can alter the prices of the cars fairly easily but it is quite difficult to change the depreciation rate because it is part of each formula. What we could do with are two cells where you input the depreciation rate for each car.

Different cars have different depreciation rates. It would be an idea to work out the accurate depreciation rates for different cars using accurate data. You can get data about prices for cars from the following web site:

www.parkers.co.uk

You may also like to look into whether the depreciation rate changes from one year to the next. If this could be built into the model it would reflect the real situation and make the model more accurate.

Worksheet 7.3

Computers in control?

There are many places where you can find computers in control. Computers can switch things on and off automatically. They can work through a process without the need for a human to be present.

Write your answers directly onto the worksheet.

Example 1 has been completed for you.

Place where you would might find computers in control	Example 1	Example 2	Example 3
In your school	Central heating system		
In your home	Washing machine		
At a fairground/theme park	To count people passing through the turnstiles		
Along a road	Fog warning system		
In a shopping centre	Controlling the barrier in the car park		

Worksheet 7.4

Describing how control is used

There are many places where control is used. For this worksheet you have to explain how control is used for each of the examples described.

To make it clear what you have to do, the first example has been done for you.

Place where you might find computers in control	Example	How control is used
In your school	Central heating system	To turn the heating on when the temperature, as measured by a sensor, falls below a set value. If the temperature rises above a different set value and the heating is on, then it will be turned off. This way the temperature remains fairly constant.
In your home	Washing machine	
At a fairground/theme park	To count people passing through the turnstiles	
Along a road	Fog warning system	
In a shopping centre	Controlling the barrier in the car park	

ICT FOR IGCSE® TEACHER RESOURCE KIT   © Oxford University Press 2012

Activity 7.1

Researching the use of robots

For this activity you have to use the Internet for research to find out about as many different uses for robots as you can.

You then have to produce a document which contains a picture of the robot along with a brief explanation as to how it is used.

To help you understand what you have to do, the first one has been done for you.

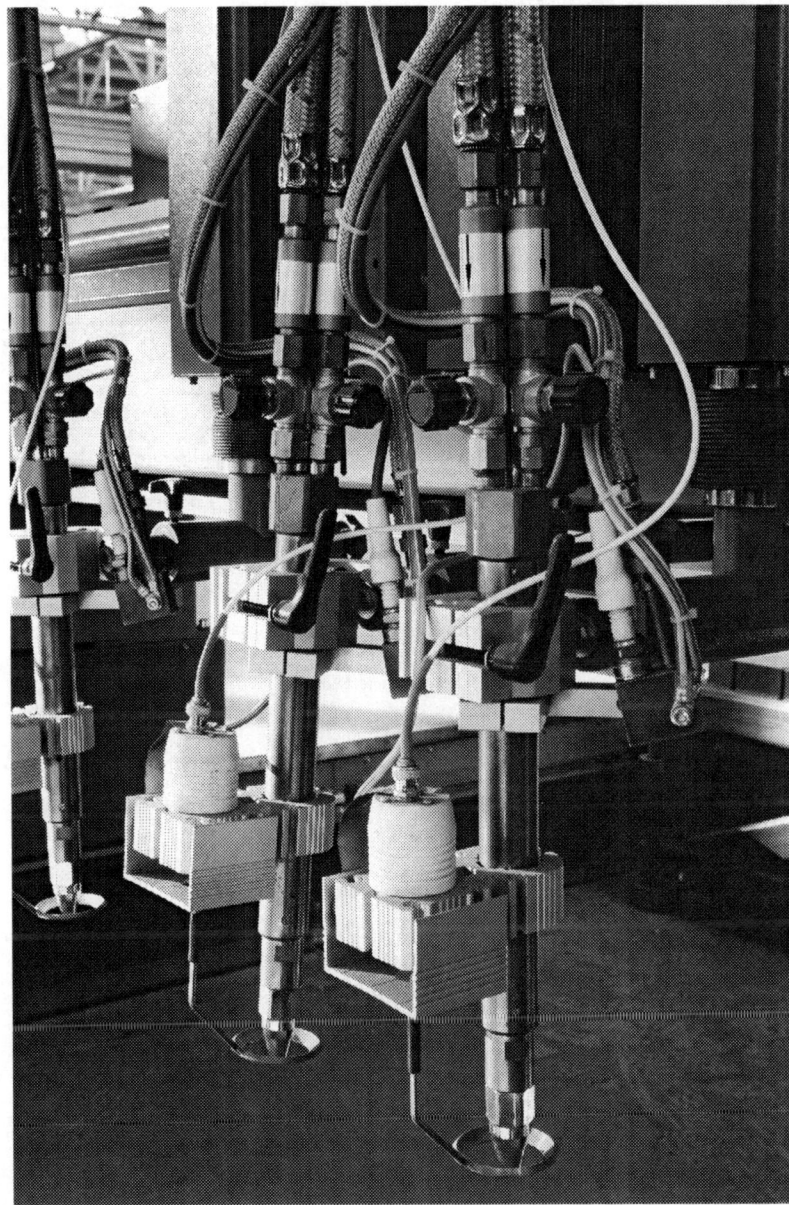

This is a robot that uses a laser to cut patterns in sheet metal. These sheets are then shaped to form the panels for car bodies. The panels are then welded together also by a robot.

Topic 7 answers

Questions A

Student book page 68

1 One mark for each correctly placed tick.

	Online	Batch	Real-time
Ordering goods using the Internet	√		
Processing the results from a questionnaire		√	
Preparing water bills automatically		√	
Controlling the flight of a plane automatically			√
Processing a payroll and printing wage slips		√	
Control of a patient life support system in a hospital			√

2 One mark for the name of the device and a brief explanation of the method used x 2.

Sequencers can be used to create and manage electronic music (1) and they include drum machines and workstations (1).

Sound wave editors can be used to alter sound waves (1). Notes can be edited, copied, cut and pasted and have special effects added (1).

MIDI (Musical Instrument Digital Interface) enables a musical instrument and a computer to communicate with each other (1). Music stored on the computer can be played back using a keyboard or other instrument (1).

3 One mark for each of two differences such as:

With batch processing the input is collected over a period of time and then batched and processed in one go (1).

Real-time processing happens immediately without any delay (1).

Real-time processing usually uses sensors to supply the input data (1).

Batch processing usually uses paper documents such as OMR forms as the input (1).

Real-time processing is usually used in control applications (1).

4 a One mark for online processing.

 b One mark for:

 While the customer is entering their details, the items they have ordered are reserved for them.

Questions B

Student book page 73

1 Marks according to the following:

No mistakes in instructions = 4 marks

1 mistake = 3 marks

2-3 mistakes = 2 marks

4-5 mistakes = 1 mark

>5 mistakes = 0 marks

FORWARD 50

RIGHT 90

FORWARD 25

PENUP

FORWARD 50

PENDOWN

FORWARD 25

RIGHT 90

FORWARD 50

RIGHT 90

FORWARD 100

2 a One mark for the name and one mark for a description of what it does x 2.

 Moisture (1) – so that the amount of water in the soil can be determined in case it is too dry (1)

 Humidity (1) – the moisture in the air can be measured so that a fine mist can be turned on or off

 Light (1) – the light is measured and controls the blinds (1)

 pH (1) – to control the acidity/alkalinity of the soil (1)

 b One mark for each advantage to a maximum of two marks.

 The system is completely automatic (1)

 No wage costs for people to water plants (1)

 c One mark for one disadvantage such as:

 High initial cost of buying the equipment

 Equipment needs to be maintained

 Equipment can malfunction which can cause plant loss

 Causes unemployment among staff who used to look after plants manually

3 One mark for each of three output devices such as:

Motor

Actuator

Heater

Lamp/Light

4 a Two sensors (one mark each) such as:

 Pressure

 Temperature

 Humidity

 Rainfall

 Light/Sun - to record hours of sunlight

 b One mark for a method and one mark for further amplification.

 The data is sent wirelessly (1) through the air and it is picked up by a receiver inside or attached to the computer (1)

ICT FOR IGCSE® TEACHER RESOURCE KIT © Oxford University Press 2012

c One mark for a method and an extra mark for further detail.

It is displayed on a small LCD screen (1) in the form of icons (such as sun/rain, etc.) (1)

It is displayed graphically (1)

Graphs are drawn to show the way the quantity measured has changed (1)

Questions C

Student book page 78

1 a One mark for each of two features:

They supply school managers with the information they need in order to make correct decisions.

They can extract specific detailed information in the form of reports.

They may allow parent access to some areas to give them information about how their child is doing.

They are used to enter and store accurate details about students, their test results and their attendance.

b One mark for a suitable advantage such as:

They reduce the workload for teachers in the classroom and in the school office

They can provide up-to-date information for parents

They can support decision making for school managers

They can tackle truancy effectively

They can be used to plan timetables

They can be used to help make budgeting decisions

c One mark for a suitable disadvantage such as:

The software is expensive to buy

Pupil data is very personal, so there must be no unauthorized access

Software is complex, so all staff need training

2 Two marks for each of two advantages such as:

The details are recorded instantly – teachers and admin staff can chase up non-attendees

Teachers have the admin burden removed – they can concentrate on teaching

Harder for students to abuse the system

Promotes health and safety – need to know who is in the school in case of an emergency

Can check attendance at each lesson

No need to physically move the registers

Takes up less space than paper-based registers

Attendance can be accessed from any computer connected to the school network

3 a One mark each for:

Credit card

Debit card

b One mark for each point made to a maximum of four marks.

Chip and PIN was introduced because all you had to do previously was sign a form (1). The signature was compared with a stored signature to verify that you were the true owner of the card (1). Signatures were easily forged (1). Now a number called a PIN is encrypted in the chip on the card (1) and the reader asks the user to enter the PIN (1). Only the true owner of the card knows the PIN (1) so this cuts down the fraudulent use of stolen cards (1).

4 a One mark for each of two ways such as:

Can be used as evidence of identity to take out loans/ credit cards

Can be used to purchase goods and services

Can be used to obtain cash from ATMs if the PIN is known

b One mark for an answer similar to the following:

Use of chip and PIN where the user has to enter a series of numbers which only they should know

Questions D

Student book page 80

1 a One mark each for the names of three sensors:

Temperature

Blood pressure

Respiration

b One mark each for two of the following:

Patient record keeping

Medical expert systems for patient diagnosis

Keeping records of staff

Payroll

Stock control

Accounts systems

Etc.

2 a Any two (one mark each) from the following:

Knowledge base

Inference engine

User interface

b One mark for one of the following:

More accurate diagnosis

Fewer mistakes as computers do not forget things

Cheaper than employing a consultant or expert

c One mark for one of the following:

Can check what they think with what the expert system thinks/get second opinion.

Patient may answer questions more truthfully if they are asked the questions by a computer.

d One mark for one of the following:

Lacks common sense

Lacks senses (e.g., can't tell pain from patient's body language)

Only as good as the person who set it up

They are very expensive to create

3 a One mark for each of two points similar to the following:

ICT systems that are designed to replace a human expert in a particular field

It uses artificial intelligence to make decisions

Decisions are based on applying a series of rules to a body of knowledge

b One mark each for two points similar to the following:

They can use the system to help them make a correct diagnosis

They can use the system to confirm a diagnosis

They can use the system when they feel they do not know enough about the illness

4 a One mark for each of two jobs similar to the following:

Doctors

Architects

Geologists

Accountants

b One mark each for two descriptions for each job referred to in part (a).

Doctors for medical diagnosis

Architects for the designing of buildings

Geologists for prospecting for minerals and oil

Accountants for giving tax advice to individuals and companies

5 One mark for the use and one mark for further explanation such as:

A financial advisor for a bank (1) who advises on the best mortgage based on their client's circumstances (1).

6 a One mark for one of the following:

More accurate diagnosis

Fewer mistakes as computers do not forget things

Cheaper than employing a consultant or expert

b One mark for one of the following:

Lacks common sense

Lacks senses (e.g., can't tell pain from patient's body language)

Only as good as the person who set it up

Questions E

Student book page 82

1 a One method for one mark such as:

Credit card

Debit card

PayPal

b One mark for each point to a maximum of two marks.

They are worried about identity theft

They are worried that their card details could be found and used fraudulently

c One mark for each point to a maximum of two marks.

Credit/debit card details are encrypted

Which means they are scrambled when sending or stored

Which prevents others understanding them

2 a One mark each for two advantages such as:

The goods are usually cheaper

It is much easier to shop around so you get the best price

You can use comparison sites to get the best price

You can see what others say about the service offered by the online store

The goods are delivered straight to your door

You can buy goods from anywhere in the world

You do not waste time looking for goods that might be out of stock

b One mark each for two disadvantages such as:

If you want the goods urgently you may still have to wait for delivery

It is sometimes necessary to see and touch what you are buying

It is hassle sending goods back

Sometime the customer service is not as good as a traditional store

There are fake stores where you pay for goods that never arrive

People may be worried about using their credit/debit card details to pay for goods owing to identity theft

c i One mark each for two suitable stores such as:

Supermarkets

Clothes stores

Bookshops

CD/DVD stores

ii One mark each for two similar to:

High street bookshops

High street record stores

Corner shops

High street travel agents

3 One mark for each detailed point (not just a name) to a maximum of six.

Goods or services are usually cheaper on the Internet.

Organizations find it cheaper to use the Internet, as they do not need as many staff, they do not need expensive premises and some of these savings can be passed to the customer.

Online catalogues can be viewed. Products can be searched for by a large number of criteria.

There is much bigger choice of products. Internet bookshops have huge stocks of books compared to a local bookshop.

Product reviews can be obtained before you buy. For example, you can see what other people, who have bought a book, say about it before you buy.

Orders can be placed on the Internet 24 hours a day, 7 days a week, 52 weeks per year.

You can buy software/music over the Internet and receive it by downloading it. This can be less effort than having to order it by mail order or by travelling to a shop to buy it.

You can use price comparison sites to ensure that the goods are bought for the best price.

Once the customer has made an initial order, the customer details such as name, address, credit card details can be stored and therefore do not need to be entered again. This makes shopping online very fast.

Supermarkets who deliver to the home also keep a shopping list of items that you order regularly so you just need to make changes in this list.

You can buy goods anywhere in the world.

Test yourself

Student book page 83

A   batch

B   batch

C   online

D   real-time

E   sensors

F   expert

G   knowledge base

H   inference engine

I   user interface

J   experts

K   question

L   diagnosis

M   cheaper

Revision questions

Student book page 83

1 **a** One mark for the name of a suitable device such as:

Washing machine

Dishwasher

Iron

Toaster

Alarm

b One mark for each of three points. Example answer for a washing machine control system might be:

Controls the flow of water into the machine

Heats the water up to the correct temperature

Uses the program to obey the set of instructions for a particular wash

Controls the pumps which pump the dirty water out of the machine

Controls when the detergent is added

Controls the spin speed

Controls how long the drier cycle is on for

Releases the door hatch when it is safe to do so

2 **a** One mark each for three advantages such as:

The details are recorded instantly – teachers and admin staff can chase up non-attendees

Teachers have the admin burden removed – they can concentrate on teaching

Harder for students to abuse the system

Promotes health and safety – need to know who is in the school in case of an emergency

Can check attendance at each lesson

No need to physically move the registers

Takes up less space than paper-based registers

Attendance can be accessed from any computer connected to the school network

b One mark for each of three disadvantages such as:

The cost – biometric methods are quite expensive

Dependence on equipment which can sometimes fail

Privacy issues if fingerprinting is used

3 One mark for each of two points similar to the following:

Welding panels or components together

Assembling components

Spraying panels/cars, etc.

Packaging goods

Deep sea repairs to oil rigs

Mowing lawns

Vacuuming carpets/floors

Etc.

4 a One mark for each service up to a maximum of three marks:

   View bank statements

   Transfer money between accounts

   Make payments for bills

   Apply for loans

b One mark for each up to a maximum of two marks:

   Worry about inputting the wrong data

   Worry about hackers accessing their banking details

   Worry about others using their account fraudulently

c One mark for one of the following:

   Worry about inputting the wrong data – bank can explain that range checks are used to check that huge amounts are not moved between accounts by mistake

   Worry about hackers accessing their banking details – explain how banking details are encrypted when passing between banks and customers

   Worry about others using their account fraudulently – explain how firewalls are used to keep personal details secure

5 One mark for each of five points which must be relevant to an Internet booking system.

   Using online processing

   Online processing means that the booking is held while you enter your personal and payment details and this prevents double booking

   You get the confirmation immediately usually as an email which you can print out

   Tickets/bookings are usually cheaper because there is no agent commission to pay

   Can read reviews on the Internet before booking

   Can use comparison sites to determine where to buy the cheapest ticket

   The tickets are sent by post to you or you can print them out, which saves time compared to picking them up

   Can book without leaving your home

   You can spend as much time as you like searching for flights, hotels, etc.

Examination questions

Student book page 84

1 One mark for each correct statement shown in bold here:

LEFT 90

REPEAT **5**

FORWARD **50**

RIGHT 72

END REPEAT

2 One mark each for four of the following:

   The user interface asks questions on the screen

   The questions relate to the geology of the area

   The user answers these questions by keying in answers

   More questions are asked on the basis of previous answers

   The system suggests likely places where oil could be found

   Percentage probabilities of finding oil in these places are shown

   Suggested information regarding the depth of the deposits is shown

   Maps showing areas where oil might be found are displayed

3 a One mark for each point to a maximum of six marks.

   Interactive screen asks user to enter details

   Details such as make, model, engine size, etc., are entered

   Questions are then asked about the problem

   Answers are input at the keyboard

   The inference engine decides on the next question based on answers to previous questions

   The knowledge base is searched using the rules base

   Problems are output on the screen

   The probabilities of each likely problem are displayed

b One mark each for two of the following:

   Mineral/oil prospecting

   Medical diagnosis

   Chess games

   For giving tax advice to individuals and companies

   For giving an insurance quote

   For careers advice/guidance

4 a One mark for each of three correct applications such as:

   Monitoring the condition of a patient in an intensive care unit in a hospital

   Monitoring the level of a river in a flood warning system

   Making an airline booking

   Purchasing goods using a site on the Internet

ICT FOR IGCSE® TEACHER RESOURCE KIT   © Oxford University Press 2012

b One mark for each of three correct applications such as:

Processing market research questionnaires

Processing multiple choice answer sheets

Producing utility bills

Producing monthly payroll for employees

Worksheet 7.3: Computers in control?

Teacher Resource Kit page 59

Place where you would might find computers in control	Example 1	Example 2	Example 3
In your school	Central heating system	Burglar alarm system	Automatic watering system for the school playing fields
In your home	Washing machine	DVD recorder	Central heating system
At a fairground/theme park	To count people passing through the turnstiles	Metal detection system for security	To control the operation of a camera on a ride
Along a road	Fog warning system	Traffic light control system	Barrier system to control the entry to a car park
In a shopping centre	Controlling the barrier in the car park	Controlling the sprinkler system in case of fire	Controlling the heating/air conditioning

Worksheet 7.4: Describing how control is used

Teacher Resource Kit page 60

Place where you might find computers in control	Example	How control is used
In your school	Central heating system	To turn the heating on when the temperature, as measured by a sensor, falls below a set value. If the temperature rises above a different set value and the heating is on, then it will be turned off. This way the temperature remains fairly constant.
In your home	Washing machine	To allow the right amount of water to enter. To heat the water up to a certain temperature, add the powder and wash for a certain time. To drain water and add more to rinse and then to empty the water and heat washing till it is dry.
At a fairground/ theme park	To count people passing through the turnstiles	To activate a counter each time the turnstile moves enough to allow a person to enter.
Along a road	Fog warning system	Light sensors will come on when there is fog obstructing the area between the light source and the light cell. When the sensor detects fog, the warning signs light up. When the fog clears, the warning signs are turned off automatically.
In a shopping centre	Controlling the barrier in the car park	When car approaches a ticket is printed and on its removal, the barrier rises. The car is detected having passed the barrier and the barrier is instructed to close.

Systems analysis and design

8

Spreadsheet cell validation checks

Here are some validation checks which are to be applied to a range of cells in a
worksheet created using spreadsheet software.

For each of the checks, give the name of the validation check and also give a brief
explanation on how the check will help prevent incorrect data being entered.

1 Validation check 1

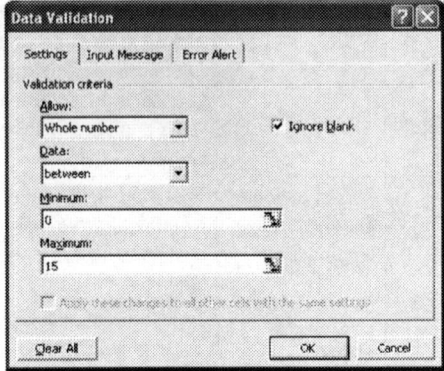

Name of validation check _____

Explanation _____

_____

2 Validation check 2

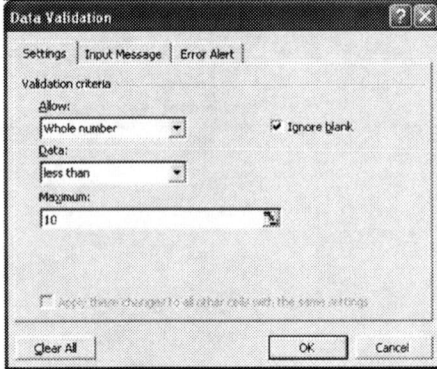

Name of validation check _____

Explanation _____

_____

ICT FOR IGCSE® TEACHER RESOURCE KIT   © Oxford University Press 2012

Worksheet 8.1 (continued)

3   Validation check 3

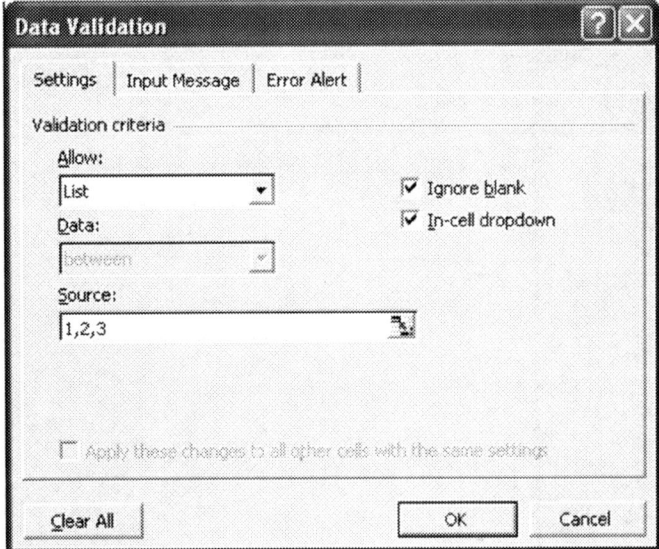

Name of validation check _____

Explanation _____

_____

4   Validation check 4

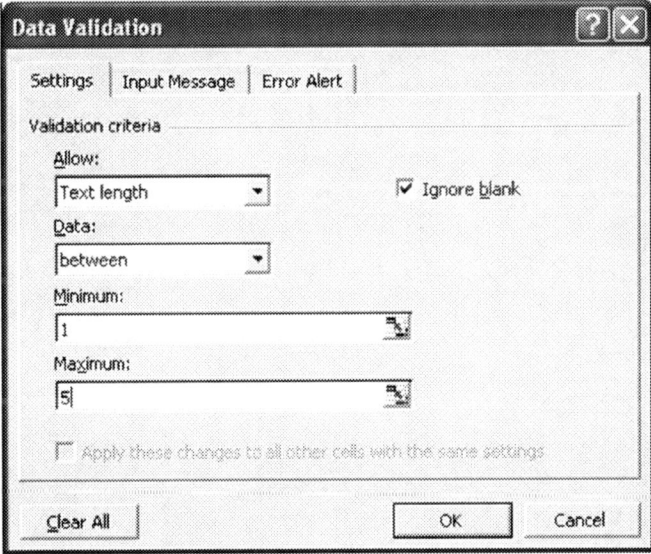

Name of validation check _____

Explanation _____

_____

Worksheet 8.1 (continued)

5 Validation check 5

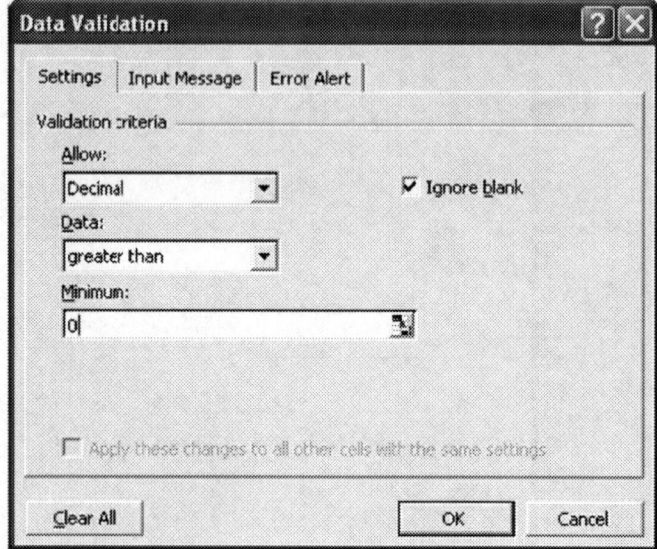

Name of validation check _____

Explanation _____

_____

ICT FOR IGCSE® TEACHER RESOURCE KIT © Oxford University Press 2012

Topic 8 answers

Questions A

Student book page 88

1 a Three marks allocated as follows:

An extra digit added at the end of a long number

That is calculated from all the other numbers

And is used to ensure that the number has been input correctly

b One mark for each example to a maximum of two marks such as:

ISBN (International Standard Book Number)

Bar code/article number on items in a supermarket

Bank account number

Utility (gas, electricity, water, phone) customer number

Part number

2 a One mark for: 12/01/3010 cannot be possible as 3010 is into the future.

b One mark for: 01/13/2000 cannot be possible as a British DoB as the max number you can have for the month is 12.

c One mark for: 30/02/1999 is not possible as there is no 30th of February.

3 a One mark for an appropriate check and one mark for the reason.

Format check (1) – only allows the letters and numbers in the format chosen (1)

Length check (1) – checks that the code contains exactly 9 characters (1)

b One mark for an appropriate check and one mark for the reason.

Range check (1) – to ensure the salary is within a certain range, e.g. greater than 0 but less than a certain salary (1)

Data type check (1) – to ensure that currency/number has been entered (1)

4 One mark for three points similar to the following:

The data might pass all the validation rules (1) but may still be wrong but because the data is allowable an error is not detected (1). For example, a date of birth might be 01/12/98 and is typed incorrectly as 12/01/98 which is still a valid date (1).

5 a One mark for each point to a maximum of three marks. Answers marked in the following way:

Some fields are compulsory such as everyone has a name (1)

Other fields can be left empty such as email address (1) as not everyone has one (1)

b One mark for suitable field for a presence check, e.g. name, address, date of birth, etc.

One mark for a suitable field where a presence check would be inappropriate such as email address, mobile phone number, works phone number, etc.

6 One mark for the name of the method and one mark for a brief description x 3.

Questionnaires (1) in order to ask questions about the old system and the desired new system (1)

Interviews (1) where people at the different levels are asked about their requirements from a system (1)

Observation (1) where the investigator sits in with someone to watch how the existing system works and learn about it (1)

Inspection of records (1) where you look at the documentation produced by the old system (1)

Questions B

Student book page 91

1 Correct order is:

Analysis

Design

Development and testing

Implementation

Documentation

Evaluation

2 a One mark for Design

b One mark for Design

c One mark for Analysis

d One mark for Evaluation

e One mark for Development and testing

3 a One mark for each of two points similar to the following:

Stop using the old system one day (1) and start using the new system the next day (1)

One mark for one advantage such as:

It requires fewer resources (people, money and equipment)

One mark for one disadvantage such as:

There is a risk that the new system may not work as expected

People may not be properly trained to cope with the new system

Test yourself

Student book page 92

A facts

B input

C implementation

D normal

E whole

F Direct changeover

G   direct changeover

H   Parallel running

I   training

J   documented

K   evaluation

Revision questions

Student book page 93

1   One mark each for two points such as:

They can use visual comparison of the data entered with the source of the data

If they match then the data can be submitted for processing

2   One mark for each point to a maximum of three marks.

Format check so date is entered in the form dd/mm/yy

Presence check to check that data has been entered

Range check to check that the number of days does not go past that for the month

Range check to check that a date of birth is not after today's date

3   **a**   One mark for 21059810J

b   One mark for each point to a maximum of two marks such as:

A check performed by a computer program

To restrict the data being entered

So that it is allowable and reasonable

So that it obeys certain rules before it is accepted

c   One mark for each of two methods. Examples include:

Range check: Check that the whole number lies between 1 and 99999999

Check that the date part lies in the range for acceptable dates, e.g. not 31/02/10 which is impossible

Check that the year of joining is not before the fitness club opened

Format check: Check to ensure that exactly 9 characters have been entered

Check to ensure that the first 8 characters are letters and the last character is a number

4   One mark for the name and one mark for an advantage/ disadvantage x 3.

Direct changeover (1) – requires fewer resources (people, money, equipment) and is simple provided nothing goes wrong (1).

Parallel running (1) – you still have the old system to rely on if things go wrong (1).

Phased implementation (1) – IT staff can deal with problems caused by a module before moving on to new modules (1).

Pilot running (1) – the implementation is on a much smaller and more manageable scale (1).

Examination questions

Student book page 93

1   One mark each for any three from the following

Direct changeover

Parallel running

Phased implementation

Pilot running

2   One mark each for four of the following:

Validation routines

List of variables

Program flowcharts

Program coding

File structures

System flowcharts

3   **a**   One mark for each correct TRUE or FALSE answer:

FALSE

FALSE

TRUE

TRUE

b   One mark each for the following four ticked items:

Data capture forms

Validation routines

File structures

Report layouts

4   **a**   One mark each for four of the following:

Borrower number/ID number

Name

Address

Postcode

Email address

Gender/Title

Date of birth

Phone number

b   One mark each for four of the following:

An easy to read font/font size

Move to first record button facility

Move to last record button facility

A font colour and background colour with plenty of contrast making it easy to read

Clearly defined area for each field

Back button or arrow

Forward button or arrow

Easy to understand instructions for entering data

No overlapping of items

Appropriate spacing for each field

Submit button to submit the details

c One mark for each point to a maximum of four marks.

Data is entered twice/the double entry of data

Computer compares both versions and only accepts the data if they are the same

Visual checking/verification

The typed in data is compared with the original data

d Three for two marks each from:

Normal data is data which lies within an acceptable range

For example, the number of books can be integer values between 1 and 6

Extreme data is data on the borderline of the accepted data

For example, the number of books 1 and 6

Abnormal data is data which is outside the acceptable range/or of the wrong data type

Example any negative number, a non-integer number, a number greater than 6, text put in instead of a number

e One mark for each tick next to the following:

Improvements can be made

Limitations of the system can be identified

To make sure the user is satisfied with the system

f One mark each for three items of technical documentation and one mark each for three items of user documentation.

User documentation

▸▸ The hardware requirements to run the system

▸▸ The operating system needed to run the software

▸▸ How to run the program/use the system

▸▸ How to log in and log out of the system

▸▸ How to perform tasks such as enter data, sort data, search for data, save data, produce printouts, etc.

▸▸ Details of sample runs

▸▸ Tutorials to help a user become familiar with using the system

▸▸ Help guides to give the user online help

▸▸ Details of input and output formats (e.g. screen layouts and print layouts)

▸▸ Error messages and how to deal with them

▸▸ Troubleshooting guide

▸▸ Frequently asked questions/FAQ /help guide

Technical documentation

▸▸ Purpose of the system

▸▸ Hardware requirements and software requirements

▸▸ A copy of the system design

▸▸ Copies of all the diagrams used to represent the system (program flowcharts, system flowcharts, network diagrams, etc.)

▸▸ Program listings/program coding

▸▸ Lists of variables used

▸▸ Details of known bugs

▸▸ Sample runs (with test data and results)

▸▸ File structures (e.g., structure of database tables, etc.)

▸▸ Validation routines used

▸▸ User interface designs

▸▸ Test plans

▸▸ Meaning of error messages

Worksheet 8.1: Spreadsheet cell validation checks

Teacher Resource Kit page 68

1 Name of validation check: Range check

Explanation: Only allows the user to enter whole numbers between and including 0 and 15.

2 Name of validation check: Range check

Explanation: Only allows the user to enter a whole number less than 10.

3 Name of validation check: Restricting the user to a list.

Explanation: Only allows the user to choose a value of 1, 2 or 3 from a drop-down list.

4 Name of validation check: Format check

Explanation: Only allows from one character to five characters inclusive to be entered.

5 Name of validation check: Range check

Explanation: Allows any number above zero to be entered.

9 Communication

Worksheet 9.1

Can you work out what the word is?

Here are some words or phrases which have been jumbled up. The words are connected with email. Can you work out what they are? There is a clue to help you.

1 **A mile**

   Hint: An electronic message.

   Answer: _____

2 **Pug or**

   Hint: Sending the same email to more than one person is sending the email to a _____.

   Answer: _____

3 **Fanatic them let**

   Hint: A file sent with an email.

   Answer: _____

4 **Far word**

   Hint: An email sent to you which you send on to others.

   Answer: _____

5 **Basked doors**

   Hint: Where you keep your list of contact email addresses.

   Answer: _____

6 **A vibe us**

   Hint: You must not use this kind of language in emails.

   Answer: _____

7 **Crab copy on**

   Hint: Copy of an email sent to others for their information.

   Answer: _____

ICT FOR IGCSE® TEACHER RESOURCE KIT   © Oxford University Press 2012

Worksheet 9.1 (continued)

8   Crop ninety

Hint: Method of keeping emails private.

Answer: _____

9   Maps

Hint: Unwanted email that you waste time deleting.

Answer: _____

10   Versus I

Hint: Emails are checked for these by your virus checker.

Answer: _____

Worksheet 9.1 (continued)

Worksheet 9.2

Creating an evaluation checklist for web sites

You have been asked to evaluate a web site. Think about the sorts of things you look for in a good web site.

Produce a checklist consisting of 20 things you should look for in a good web site.

1 _____

_____

2 _____

_____

3 _____

_____

4 _____

_____

5 _____

_____

6 _____

_____

7 _____

_____

8 _____

_____

9 _____

_____

10 _____

_____

11 _____

_____

12 _____

_____

ICT FOR IGCSE® TEACHER RESOURCE KIT

Worksheet 9.2 (continued)

13 _____
_____

14 _____
_____

15 _____
_____

16 _____
_____

17 _____
_____

18 _____
_____

19 _____
_____

20 _____
_____

Worksheet 9.2 (continued)

Activity 9.1

Practising sending email

Take a look at the email facility that you are familiar with.

1 Set up an address book with the names and email addresses of at least 10 of your friends or relatives. Use this address book to send an email to one of your friends.

2 Explain briefly what an address book is and how it can be useful to someone who uses email.

3 Set up a mailing list to send the same email message to at least four of your friends. After you have learnt how to do this write a list explaining the steps you took so that you can refer to this in the future.

4 Explain briefly what a mailing list is and how it is useful to someone who uses email.

5 Set up a file to send with an email. This file could be a word-processed document, a spreadsheet, an image and attach the file to an email and send it to one of your friends. Send an email message with the file to tell them that you have sent them a file and what it consists of.

6 Explain the steps involved in attaching a file to an email.

ICT FOR IGCSE® TEACHER RESOURCE KIT   © Oxford University Press 2012

Activity 9.2

Explaining the features of email

For this activity you have to explain some of the features of email using a screen shot.

A screen shot is a picture of the screen you are looking at. To perform a screen shot of the screen you are looking at you press the 'Prt Scr' key on the keyboard. To take a screenshot of the currently selected window, hold down the 'Alt' key and press 'Prt Scr'.

A copy of the entire screen is held in the clipboard and this allows you to paste it into a document like this.

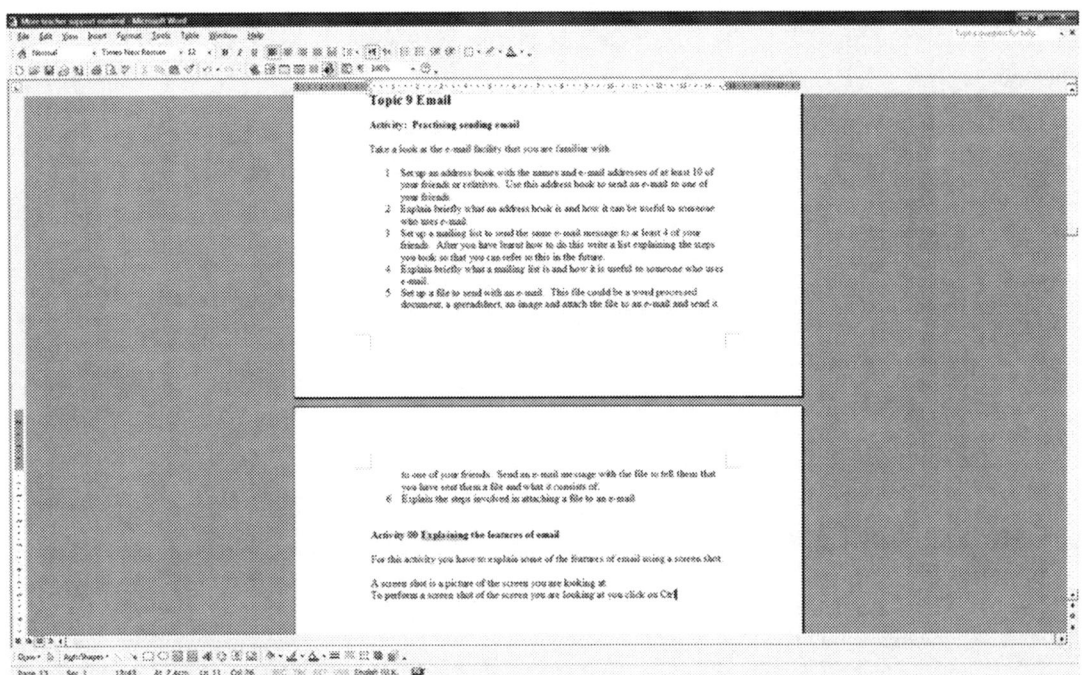

You have to do this for the opening screen of the email package you use.

You now have to paste this into a word-processed document.

When you have done this you need to explain the various parts/features of the email package by making use of arrows and text boxes. This process is called annotation.

When you have completed this work save a copy and print the work out to show to your teacher/lecturer.

Topic 9 answers

Activity 9.6

Student book page 100

1 The common toad

2 The foxglove

3 Knee cap

4 Spain

5 Seven Ancient Wonders of the world are:

  Great Pyramid at Giza

  Hanging Gardens of Babylon

  Statue of Zeus at Olympia

  Temple of Artemis at Ephesus

  Mausoleum at Halicarnassus

  Colossus of Rhodes

  Lighthouse at Alexandria

6 21st July 1969

7 Brazil

8 Red, blue, yellow and green.

9 Cheetah

10 Malaysia

Worksheet 9.1: Can you work out what the word is?

Teacher Resource Kit page 74

1 Email

2 Group

3 File attachment

4 Forward

5 Address book

6 Abusive

7 Carbon copy

8 Encryption

9 Spam

10 Viruses

Worksheet 9.2: Creating an evaluation checklist for web sites

Teacher Resource Kit page 76

Here are some of the many possible criteria:

Is the content of the site accurate?

Is the content easy to understand?

Is the content free from spelling and grammatical errors?

Can you tell when the site was last updated?

Is the content kept up-to-date?

Does the site have a search facility?

Is the site easy to navigate?

Do the pages appear overcrowded?

Has colour been used to good effect?

Have appropriate images been included?

Did the site take a long time to load?

Have any annoying animations been included?

Have suitable fonts and font sizes been included?

Do all the links work?

If the links are followed, do they link to relevant and interesting material?

Have long scrolling pages been avoided?

Are there too many pop-up advertisements on the pages?

Is there any general useful information such as the weather on the page?

Is the information on the page in a sensible order?

Does it tell you how many people have viewed the page (i.e. does it include a counter)?

10 Document production

Topic 10 answers

Activity 10.5

Student book page 114

1 Serif
2 Sans serif
3 Sans serif
4 Serif
5 Serif
6 Sans serif
7 Sans serif
8 Sans serif
9 Serif
10 Serif

Data manipulation

Topic 11 answers

Activity 11.6

Student book page 139

1 Query design

Field:	[Surname]	[Forename]	[Sex]	[Position]
Table:	tblEmployees	tblEmployees	tblEmployees	tblEmployees
Sort:				
Show:	✓	✓	✓	✓
Criteria:			= "F"	=Programmer
or:				

Results of query

Surname	Forename	Sex	Position
Karunakaram	Viveta	F	Programmer
Sadik	Sally	F	Programmer
Liu	Rachel	F	Programmer
Jackson	Samantha	F	Programmer
Singh	Praba	F	Programmer
*			

2 Query design

Field:	ID;	[Forename]	[Surname]	[Sex]	[DOB]	[No of IGCSEs]	[IGCSE Maths]	[IGCSE English]	[Position]	[Salary (US $)]	[Full or part time]	[Driving licence held]
Table:	tblEmployees	tblEmployees	tblEmployees	tblEmployees	tblEmployees	tblEmployees	tblEmployees	tblEmployees	tblEmployees	tblEmployees	tblEmployees	tblEmployees
Sort:												
Show:	✓	✓	✓	✓	✓	✓	✓	✓	✓	✓	✓	✓
Criteria:											= "P"	
or:												

Results of query

ID	Forename	Surname	Sex	DOB	No of IGCSEs	IGCSE Maths	IGCSE English	Position	Salary (US $)	Full or part time	Driving licence held
5	Viveta	Karunakaram	F	09/10/1978	5	Yes	Yes	Programmer	16500	P	Yes
13	Sho Ling	Wong	F	17/06/1978	9	Yes	Yes	Animator	28000	P	No
15	Rachel	Hughes	F	16/09/1991	0	No	No	Network administrator	34200	P	No
17	Marzena	Jankowski	F	31/12/1995	2	No	Yes	Admin clerk	32000	P	Yes
20	James	Murphy	M	30/06/1964	4	No	Yes	Admin clerk	26000	P	No
21	Rajan	Uppal	M	22/08/1977	5	Yes	Yes	Web designer	14000	P	Yes
25	Rupinder	Singh	M	29/05/1990	6	Yes	No	Finance clerk	24900	P	No
27	Osama	Diad	M	03/11/1993	2	No	No	Trainee network engineer	23000	P	No
31	Fay	Roy	F	09/10/1988	8	Yes	Yes	Receptionist	21300	P	No
32	Robert	Marley	M	17/05/1965	0	No	No	Marketing administrator	21000	P	No
35	Mia	Hamm	M	06/11/1978	2	No	Yes	Finance clerk	12000	P	No
37	Michael	Hazat	M	01/03/1995	6	No	Yes	Programmer	19000	P	Yes
38	Kevin	Doyle	M	10/09/1992	1	No	No	Web designer	17000	P	Yes
*	[New]											

3 Query design

Field:	[Surname]	[Forename]	[Salary (US $)]	[Sex]
Table:	tblEmployees Query1	tblEmployees Query1	tblEmployees Query1	tblEmployees Query1
Sort:				
Show:	✓	✓	✓	✓
Criteria:			< 20000	
or:				

Results of query

Surname	Forename	Salary (US $)	Sex
Karunakaram	Viveta	16500	F
Uppal	Rajan	14000	M
Hamm	Mia	12000	M
Hazat	Michael	19000	M
Doyle	Kevin	17000	M
*			

4 Query design

Field:	[Surname]	[Forename]	[Position]
Table:	tblEmployees	tblEmployees	tblEmployees
Sort:			
Show:	✓	✓	✓
Criteria:			= "Programmer"
or:			= "Web designer"

Results of query

Surname	Forename	Position
Singh	Yasmin	Web designer
Bugalia	Mohamed	Programmer
Karunakaram	Viveta	Programmer
Singh	Yuvraj	Web designer
Sadik	Sally	Programmer
Borade	Nakul	Web designer
Liu	Rachel	Programmer
Uppal	Rajan	Web designer
Nordin	Abdullah	Web designer
Jackson	Samantha	Programmer
Hazat	Michael	Programmer
Doyle	Kevin	Web designer
Singh	Praba	Programmer
*		

5 Query design

Field:	[Surname]	[Forename]	[Position]	[No of IGCSEs]
Table:	tblEmployees	tblEmployees	tblEmployees	tblEmployees
Sort:				
Show:	✓	✓	✓	✓
Criteria:				<=3
or:				

Results of query

Surname	Forename	Position	No of IGCSEs
Singh	Yasmin	Web designer	3
Gomaz	Alex	Artist	0
Schastok	Bianca	Systems analyst	0
Pathak	Vyoma	Technician	1
Hughes	Rachel	Network administrator	0
Jankowski	Marzena	Admin clerk	2
Singh	Bishen	Assistant network manager	0
Diad	Osama	Trainee network engineer	2
Nordin	Abdullah	Web designer	2
Marley	Robert	Marketing administrator	0
Hamm	Mia	Finance clerk	2
Doyle	Kevin	Web designer	1
*			

6 Query design

Field:	[Surname]	[Position]	[Salary (US $)]
Table:	tblEmployees	tblEmployees	tblEmployees
Sort:			
Show:	✓	✓	✓
Criteria:		Not "Programmer"	
or:			

Results of query

Surname	Position	Salary (US $)
Singh	Web designer	43000
Nanas	Network manager	67000
Singh	Web designer	47000
Karwad	Systems analyst	54000
Gomaz	Artist	41000
Schastok	Systems analyst	56500
Pathak	Technician	41000
Borade	Web designer	45000
Wong	Animator	28000
Burns	Security analyst	52000
Hughes	Network administrator	34200
Hughes	Director	78000
Jankowski	Admin clerk	32000
Singh	Assistant network manager	39500
Ncube	Director	87000
Murphy	Admin clerk	26000
Uppal	Web designer	14000
Zadeh	Trainee analyst	23000
Fortuni	Trainee analyst	26000
Fortuni	Technician	27000
Singh	Finance clerk	24900
Wilson	Finance clerk	37000
Diad	Trainee network engineer	23000
Fathy	Network engineer	41800
Sheata	Network engineer	43000
Nordin	Web designer	42000
Hoy	Receptionist	21300
Marley	Marketing administrator	21000
Al Sheikh	Marketing administrator	27600
Hamm	Finance clerk	12000
Doyle	Web designer	17000
Singh	Finance clerk	23000
*		

ICT FOR IGCSE® TEACHER RESOURCE KIT   © Oxford University Press 2012

7 Query design

Field:	[Surname]	[Forename]	[Position]
Table:	tblEmployees	tblEmployees	tblEmployees
Sort:			
Show:	☑	☑	☑
Criteria:			Like "*clerk"
or:			

Results of query

Surname ▾	Forename ▾	Position ▾
Jankowski	Marzena	Admin clerk
Murphy	James	Admin clerk
Singh	Rupinder	Finance clerk
Wilson	Emily	Finance clerk
Hamm	Mia	Finance clerk
Singh	Anesha	Finance clerk
*		

8 Query design

Field:	[Surname]	[Position]	[Salary (US $)]
Table:	tblEmployees	tblEmployees	tblEmployees
Sort:			
Show:	☑	☑	☑
Criteria:		Like "*clerk"	
or:		Like "*analyst"	

Results of query

Surname ▾	Position ▾	Salary (US $) ▾
Karwad	Systems analyst	54000
Schastok	Systems analyst	56500
Burns	Security analyst	52000
Jankowski	Admin clerk	32000
Murphy	Admin clerk	26000
Zadeh	Trainee analyst	23000
Fortuni	Trainee analyst	26000
Singh	Finance clerk	24900
Wilson	Finance clerk	37000
Hamm	Finance clerk	12000
Singh	Finance clerk	23000
*		

9 Query design

Field:	[Surname]	[Position]	[Salary (US $)]
Table:	tblEmployees	tblEmployees	tblEmployees
Sort:	Ascending		
Show:	☑	☑	☑
Criteria:			> = 40000
or:			

Results of query

Surname	Position	Salary (US $)
Borade	Web designer	45000
Bugalia	Programmer	48000
Burns	Security analyst	52000
Fathy	Network engineer	41800
Gomaz	Artist	41000
Hughes	Director	78000
Karwad	Systems analyst	54000
Nanas	Network manager	67000
Ncube	Director	87000
Nordin	Web designer	42000
Pathak	Technician	41000
Schastok	Systems analyst	56500
Sheata	Network engineer	43000
Singh	Web designer	47000
Singh	Web designer	43000
*		

10 Query design

Field:	[Forename]	[Surname]	[Position]	[Sex]	[Salary (US $)]
Table:	tblEmployees	tblEmployees	tblEmployees	tblEmployees	tblEmployees
Sort:					
Show:	☑	☑	☑	☐	☐
Criteria:				"F"	>30000
or:					

Results of query

Forename	Surname	Position
Yasmin	Singh	Web designer
Amor	Nanas	Network manager
Sally	Sadik	Programmer
Bianca	Schastok	Systems analyst
Vyoma	Pathak	Technician
Rachel	Liu	Programmer
Chloe	Burns	Security analyst
Rachel	Hughes	Network administrator
Grace	Hughes	Director
Marzena	Jankowski	Admin clerk
Emily	Wilson	Finance clerk
Samantha	Jackson	Programmer
*		

ICT FOR IGCSE® TEACHER RESOURCE KIT   © Oxford University Press 2012

12 Integration

Activity 12.1

Collecting objects to integrate into documents

For this activity you have to produce a set of objects for **one** of the following:

▸▸ A poster for a sporting event

▸▸ A web page for a virtual tour of your neighbourhood

▸▸ A web page which is an introduction to your family.

You only need to collect the objects and store them in a suitable folder and subfolder structure. Do not produce either the final graphics or the web page/poster.

What you need to collect

You need to collect objects such as:

▸▸ Text which is typed into word-processing software and then saved or copy and pasted from the Internet

▸▸ Pictures/Photographs

▸▸ Plans/Maps/Diagrams

▸▸ Symbols/Signs/Logos

▸▸ Patterns/Textures for backgrounds/pictures, etc.

▸▸ Examples of suitable fonts

▸▸ Unusual colours or effects you would like to use.

Note: You only need to include examples from the above list if they are appropriate to your design.

Activity 12.2

Creating a short article about weather in your local area

You have some friends visiting you and your country from another part of the world. They are not sure what clothes to pack. They have asked you to supply them with some information about the weather over a whole year in your country.

Because you do not have a lot of time to prepare this material, you have decided to collect most of the material from the Internet and then integrate it into a word-processed document. This word-processed document could then be sent as a file attachment to an email.

Here are the steps you will need to take:

1 Create a new document in a word-processing package.

2 Search for a table of maximum and minimum temperatures over a year using the Internet.

3 Create a suitable table using your word-processing software to hold the data you have found.

4 Copy and paste the data from the Internet into the table in the word-processed document.

5 Using the word-processing software to tidy up the data in the table if needed and create suitable column headings.

6 It has been decided to produce a graph as well as a table in the document. Select the data in the table by copying it and then open a spreadsheet and paste the data into the cells.

7 Using spreadsheet software create a suitable graph or graphs to illustrate the weather details. Ensure that any axes are suitably labelled and that you have a title for each graph/chart.

8 Once you have produced suitable graphs/charts you then have to copy and paste them into the word-processed document, just below the table.

9 Add suitable text to the document explaining the weather in your country. You can add the text by typing it in yourself or copy and paste it from a suitable web site or use a combination of the two.

10 Add a footer to the document containing the page number, your name and date on which the document was produced. You are free to choose the positioning of these items.

11 Carefully spellcheck and proof-read your document and correct any errors you spot.

12 Save the document using a suitable filename and print a copy out.

Output data

Activity 13.1

Producing a guide to printing a draft document

For this activity you are required to produce a word-processed quick guide to printing a draft document. You will need to produce screenshots with instructions on how to produce a draft document.

Activity 13.2

Producing evidence of slide transitions and animations

In the examination you will probably have to produce a slide presentation.

In order for this slide presentation to be marked, you will have to produce certain printouts.

For this activity you are required to explain how you would provide printout evidence for each of the following:

▸▸ A copy of the presentation slides that includes the presenter notes

▸▸ A copy of the audience notes

▸▸ Evidence of the animation of bullet points

▸▸ Evidence of the animation of slide transitions

A good way to do this is to use a presentation that you have already prepared (for ICT or a completely different subject) and then try to supply each item in the bulleted list above and then write a short paragraph explaining what you did.

14 Data analysis

Questions on spreadsheets, spreadsheet models and flat-file databases

1 Give the names of **two** functions that can be used in spreadsheets. [2]

2 Explain the difference between a relative cell address and an absolute cell address. [2]

3 One of the following formulae contains a mistake. Which one is it? [1]

	Put a tick in **one** box only
=b3*c7	
=A1+A2+A3	
Sum(A1:A14)	
=C3*F4	

4 A book store uses a database to store details about the books in stock. Part of this database is shown below:

Stock number	Book title	Book type	Number in stock
126745454	HTML for beginners	Computing	22
213331233	ICT made easy	Computing	15
225664461	A history of the World Cup	Sport	32
300123232	Tennis for beginners	Sport	26
812323333	Film stars of the 1920s	Film	12

a How many fields are there in this part of the database? [1]

b How many records are there in this part of the database? [1]

c Give the name of the field that is already sorted in order. [1]

d The records shown are to be sorted in ascending order of number in stock.
What will be the book title of the first record in the database after it has been sorted? [1]

e Which field would be the key field? [1]

f Name and describe the most suitable validation check which would be carried out on the Number in stock field. [3]

5 A shop owner uses a spreadsheet to calculate his profits. This is part of the spreadsheet:

	A	B	C	D	E	F	G
1	Manufacturer	Product name	Number of items in stock	Cost price	Selling price	Profit	Total profit
2	IMP	Spade	232	$34.50	$42.45	$7.95	$1,844.40
3	IMP	Fork	267	$30.95	$35.50	$4.55	$1,214.85
4	Bullan	Hoe	189	$26.75	$32.45	$5.70	$1,077.30
5	Spearing	Trowel	167	$19.85	$23.75	$3.90	$651.30
6	Sprearing	Spade	122	$17.85	$21.25	$3.40	$414.80
7							
8		Total in stock	977		Overall profit		$5,202.65
9							
10							

a Give the cell reference of the cell that contains 167. [1]

    b Give the cell reference of a cell that contains
       text data.   [1]

    c Write down the formula which should go in cell F2.   [1]

    d Write down the formula which should go in cell C8.   [1]

    e A similar formula should go in cell G8.

       Describe how somebody could get this formula in G8 without typing it in.   [2]

    f This is an example of a financial model.

       Give two examples of computer models, other than financial models.   [2]

6 A teacher has produced the following spreadsheet that records the marks in four examinations and works out the total mark.

	A	B	C	D	E	F	G
1	Forename	Surname	Exam 1	Exam 2	Exam 3	Exam 4	Total
2	Amy	Hughes	56	34	67	78	235
3	Jack	Danniels	56	58	45	56	215
4	John	Harris	77	89	77	89	332
5	Asif	Khan	57	79	75	78	289
6	Ian	Handley	33	75	85	88	281
7	Daisy	Doyle	74	45	88	90	297
8	Jane	Adams	90	89	55	87	321
9	Danielle	Prescott	87	90	77	77	331
10	Harry	Sumner	99	100	88	90	377
11	Jane	Hughes	45	56	65	66	232
12	Adam	Jackson	55	50	45	54	204
13							
14							
15	Average mark for all pupils						

    a Which one of the following formulae would correctly give the total in cell G2? [1]

       A   =SUM(C2:C12)

       B   =C2+D2+E2+F2+G2

       C   =SUM(C2:F2)

       D   =SUM(C2*F2)

    b Give a suitable formula to put into cell D15 to calculate the average of the numbers in column G.   [1]

    c Which cell formatting feature has been used in Column A?   [1]

    d The text in the spreadsheet 'Average mark for all pupils' has cell formatting applied to it. Give the name of the cell formatting used.   [1]

    e Give **two** advantages of using spreadsheet software rather than work the totals out using pen, paper and a calculator.   [2]

ICT FOR IGCSE® TEACHER RESOURCE KIT   © Oxford University Press 2012

Topic 14 answers

Questions on spreadsheets, spreadsheet models and flat-file databases

1 One mark each for two functions such as:

Average

Maximum

Minimum

Sum

Medium

Mode

Round

Roundup

Rank

Count

CountA

Etc.

2 One mark for each difference.

Absolute reference: a reference to a cell used in a formula where, when the formula is copied to a new address, the cell address does not change.

Relative reference: when a cell is used in a formula and the formula is copied to a new address, the cell address changes to take account of the formula's new position.

3 One mark for the following correct answer:

	Put a tick in **one** box only
=b3*c7	
=A1+A2+A3	
Sum(A1:A14)	√
=C3*F4	

4 a One mark for 4

b One mark for 5

c One mark for Stock number

d One mark for Film stars of the 1920s

e One mark for Stock number

f One mark for the name Range check

Two marks for:

Will check that the number being entered lies within an acceptable range (1)

So that numbers that are too small or too large are rejected (1)

5 a c5

b Any cell address containing words (e.g. a2)

c =e2-d2

d =sum(c2:c6) or =c2+c3+c4+c5+c6

e Click on the cell containing the formula to be copied, right click and select copy (1)

Move to cell G8 and paste the formula by right clicking and selecting paste (1)

f Two distinctly different non-financial models such as:

Model of queues at supermarket tills

Model to show the amount of electricity used by a family

A traffic light model to work out the best timings for the lights

A flight simulator to train pilots

6 a One mark for: **C** or **=SUM(C2:F2)**

b One mark for =AVERAGE(G2:G12)

c One mark for right justify/right align

d One mark for 'cell merging'

e One mark for each point to a maximum of two marks:

Automatic recalculation

Accurate calculations

Can perform 'what if' investigations

Can easily produce graphs and charts

It is easy to reuse the spreadsheet

15 Web site authoring

Questions on web site authoring

1 a A teacher has asked some pupils to produce a school magazine but the pupils
have suggested to the teacher that it might be better to create a web site.

Describe **three** features a web site would have which hard copy would not. [3]

b The web site will need to contain pictures of pupils in lessons.

Explain how these pictures could be obtained and what might need to be done to
the pictures to make them suitable for including on a web site. [5]

c Give **three** disadvantages of having a web site instead of hard copy. [3]

2 Choose which one of the following **best** matches the description in the
left-hand column of the table below. Write your answer in the space provided. [5]

browser	transition	editor	
podcast	HTML	hyperlink	tags

Description	Term best matching
Special code that is used for making web pages.	
An icon, graphic, or word on a document (slide or web page) that, when clicked with the mouse, opens another slide or web page.	
Software that is responsible for requesting text and graphics stored on servers and then assembling them for display.	
Software used for creation and editing of text.	
Special markers used in HTML to tell the computer what to do with the text.	

ICT FOR IGCSE® TEACHER RESOURCE KIT   © Oxford University Press 2012

Topic 15 answers

Questions on web site authoring

1 a One mark each for three of the following:

Links – you can move between the web pages faster

Multimedia – can use sound and video to add interest

More up-to-date information – to update a school magazine would involve re-publishing it

Web sites can be updated on a weekly or even daily basis

Ability of a user of the web site to post their own comments

b One mark each for five of the following:

Photographs of pupils working can be taken using a digital camera

Image files can be edited using image editing software

They can have size, brightness, contrast, etc., altered

The image file can be cropped so that unwanted parts of the image are removed

The image can be distorted slightly to fit a space on a web page

The file format for an image can be changed so that it is faster to load

c One mark each for three disadvantages similar to the following:

A web site is more complex to create

You need Internet access to view the web site and this may not always be available

You need a computer or other device to view the web site

2 One mark for each correct answer.

Description	Term best matching
Special code that is used for making web pages.	HTML
An icon, graphic, or word on a document (slide or web page) that, when clicked with the mouse, opens another slide or web page.	Hyperlink
Software that is responsible for requesting text and graphics stored on servers and then assembling them for display.	Browser
Software used for creation and editing of text.	Editor
Special markers used in HTML to tell the computer what to do with the text.	Tags

16 Presentation authoring

Worksheet 16.1

How much do you know about the presentation software PowerPoint?

You will be using the presentation software PowerPoint in your course. You will probably know quite a lot about the software already. See how much basic knowledge you have by answering the following questions on this worksheet.

What does each of the following do?

1 Arial ▾ _____

2 ≡ _____

3 A˙ _____

4 Design _____

5 _____

6 _____

7 _____

8 _____

9 A ▾ _____

10 _____

96

Questions on presentation authoring

1 The creator of a presentation for children aimed at helping them learn their times tables wants to make it interesting for them. They decide to use slide transitions and animation to help.

   a Explain what is meant by a slide transition. [1]

   b Explain what is meant by an animation. [1]

2 A tourist information office decides to produce a self-running presentation on all the local attractions.

   a Define each of the following functions of the presentation software, and explain, using an appropriate example, how each function could be used in this situation. [4]

      i Master slides

      ii Slide transitions

   b Animations can be added to a presentation. Describe **one** type of animation that is provided as part of the presentation software. [2]

3 Presentation software can be used to present information to a large number of people at a sales conference.

   a Explain what is meant by presentation software. [2]

   b Describe **three** features of presentation software that can be used to keep the audience interested in the information being presented. [3]

4 Joshua has to produce a presentation in front of his class. For this presentation he decides to use presentation software.

   Describe **three** features of presentation software that will make the presentation more interesting to the class. [6]

5 When using an image on a presentation slide you often have to alter/manipulate the image in some way.

   Describe **three** different ways in which an image can be manipulated before being placed on a presentation slide. [6]

Topic 16 answers

Worksheet 16.1: How much do you know about the presentation software PowerPoint?

Teacher Resource Kit page 96

1 Arial   Changes the font type

2 ≡   Centres

3 A   Increases the font size

4 Design   Slide design (pick a template, colour scheme or animation)

5   Create tables or borders

6   Create a text box

7   Slide sorter view

8   Slide show starting from the current slide

9 A ▾   Font colour

10   Bullet points

Questions on presentation authoring

1 a One mark for an answer similar to: The way one slide is replaced by another on the screen.

b One mark for: The movement of a piece of text or graphic on the screen.

2 a i One mark for the definition and one mark for the example.

Master slides are used to place objects and set styles on each slide. Using master slides you can format titles, backgrounds, colour schemes, slide numbers, etc. By changing an item such as a font size on the master slide, it will change all those slides based on it automatically. This saves having to make changes on each slide. An example would be to have a slide, containing the logo for a tourist information office, a graphic, a certain background colour and some text in headers and footers such as today's date, the page number, the name of the person who created the presentation, etc.

ii One mark for the definition and one mark for the example.

Slide transitions refer to the way slides can appear on the screen or it can refer to the way individual components such as text or graphics appear on the screen. For example, the slide for a different attraction could appear from different directions to add impact to the slide show.

b One mark for each point made to a maximum of two marks such as:

One mark for explanation of animation (e.g. pinwheel, fading, etc.)

One mark for explanation of how titles or bullet points are added

3 a One mark for two points similar to the following:

Software that is used to present information to others (1). Usually a computer screen or data projector is used to present the information as a series of slides (1). The slides give the audience a summary of the information being presented (1).

b One mark for each of three features such as:

Addition of graphics/pictures/images (1)

Interesting page layout (1)

Good structure by using different font sizes, font types and font styles (1)

Use of animation (1)

Use of narration/sound/music (1)

Use of video (1)

The use of slide transitions/special effects which move content onto a slide (1)

4 One mark for the feature and one mark for an explanation as to how it will make the presentation more interesting x 3.

Inclusion of video (1). The video can be used to show moving images and sound which will add more interest (1).

Inclusion of animation (1). The text can be animated so that it moves onto the page in a spectacular way (1).

Inclusion of images (1). Can be used to illustrate a point (1).

Include sound/music (1). Can record a narration to go with the slides (1).

5   One mark for the name and one mark for a short description x 3.

▶▶ Resizing (i.e. made bigger or smaller in order to fit a certain space on the slide).

▶▶ Positioning (i.e. the image needs to be selected and dragged into the correct position)

▶▶ Cropping (i.e. only using part of the image).

▶▶ Copying (i.e. so that the same image can be used in different places).

▶▶ Changing the image contrast (i.e. adjusting the difference between the light and dark parts of the image).

▶▶ Changing the brightness (i.e. making the whole image lighter or darker).

Case studies

Although case studies do not feature in the examinations, they can be used with your students to add breadth and interest to their studies. Case studies are included here which help your students consolidate their learning.

Case study 1

Identity fraud

At a recent trial five people who had stolen the identities of the living and the dead were found guilty of fraud and were sentenced to between 4 and 8 years in prison.

The gang forged driving licences, pay slips and utility bills (e.g. gas and electricity bills) to steal the real identities of people who lived at properties which were now vacant.

The gang stole the identities of 60 people around the country and used them to take out bank loans, overdrafts and credit cards.

The money they made was huge and the ringleader drove a $250,000 sports car and wore a $45,000 watch.

The judge when passing sentence said that the crimes were complex and sophisticated.

Questions

1   Identity theft has risen by a large amount over recent years.
    Give two pieces of advice to a person who does not want to be a victim of identity
    theft/fraud.   *(2 marks)*

2   Once a person's identity has been stolen, the thief can do several things with the new identity.
    Describe one thing that the thief can do that will affect the victim.   *(2 marks)*

ICT FOR IGCSE® TEACHER RESOURCE KIT   © Oxford University Press 2012

Case study 2

Home copying

The music industry has been hit hard by Internet file sharing and CDs being copied.

Over half of young people copy the music on their hard drives to friends and they also copy CDs. This deprives the music industry of a large amount of money and prevents them investing in new artists.

The music industry has tended to focus its attention on the file sharing sites which allow people to illegally copy music or video files between each other. Such sites allow users to use peer-to-peer networking to transfer files.

It has been estimated that 95% of young people are illegally copying music and that only one in twenty downloads is legal. It is interesting to note that the average 18-24 year old keeps around £750 of unpaid-for music on their MP3 player. Multiply this by the number in this age group and you have a massive amount of money being lost to the music industry.

An organization called the BMR (British Music Rights) helps the music industry take the owners of file sharing sites to court but it is worried that individuals who know that file copying is illegal, still do it.

The worry is that professional musicians and songwriters will reach the point where they cannot make a living and they will have to give up. This will be to the detriment of everyone who enjoys listening to music.

Questions

1   Music can be downloaded legally or illegally.

   a   Explain what the term 'downloading' means. *(2 marks)*

   b   Describe one situation where music can be downloaded legally and one situation where music can be downloaded illegally. *(2 marks)*

2   Anyone who is involved in the music industry is affected by illegal downloads.

   a   Explain one way in which a recording company would be affected by these illegal downloads. *(1 mark)*

   b   Explain one way in which a musician, group or singer would be affected by these illegal downloads. *(1 mark)*

3   In the UK, The Copyright Designs and Patents Act makes it an offence to illegally download or copy music. It forbids the copying of other things as well. Give the names of two different things which are copied illegally. *(2 marks)*

Case study 3

How using social networking sites might cause you health problems

You already know that using computers can cause a number of health problems such as back ache, repetitive strain injury (RSI) and eye strain. Some doctors think that the use of social networking sites could cause serious health problems.

Increased isolation from people could raise your risk of serious health problems because of lack of face-to-face contact. It may impair immune responses and alter hormones.

Social networking sites allow people to keep in touch with friends over the web. But although they are supposed to bring people together, they may be doing the reverse. The hours spent communicating with 'virtual' friends is reducing the amount of time spent with real people.

More people are also teleworking, which means that most of their communication with other workers is via email, VoIP and videoconferencing.

One doctor has stated that, 'Levels of hormones such as the "cuddle chemical" oxytocin, which promotes bonding, altered according to whether people were in close contact or not'. He went on to say that, 'There does seem to be a difference between "real presence" and the virtual variety'.

Questions

1 One health problem caused by the use of computers is RSI.
   Give the meaning of the term RSI.

   (1 mark)

2 Explain two things you can do using a social networking site. *(2 marks)*

3 Many teleworkers use ICT systems that mean they do not have to meet face-to-face
   (i.e. in person).

   a Explain what is meant by teleworking. *(2 marks)*

   b Many teleworkers make use of VoIP. Give the meaning of the abbreviation VoIP. *(1 mark)*

   c Explain one reason why many teleworkers choose to use VoIP. *(1 mark)*

   d Teleworkers often make use of a system which allows them to conduct 'virtual'
      face-to-face meetings. Give the name of this system and explain how it benefits
      teleworkers. *(3 marks)*

4 Explain why some doctors reckon that lack of social contact with real people might cause some
   health problems. *(2 marks)*

ICT FOR IGCSE® TEACHER RESOURCE KIT   © Oxford University Press 2012

Case study 4

Cyber warfare

Most developed countries are totally dependent on their ICT systems, and the loss of such systems could do serious damage to the infrastructure of countries.

For example, could you imagine the loss of the Internet for a lengthy period or the loss of the entire mobile phone network? What about the erasure of all the health information on health service computers? Or the erasure of tax information so that the government could not collect money to pay for schools, hospitals, the police, etc.?

In many ways attacks on ICT systems could do a lot more damage than a series of terrorist bombs or even a war using conventional weapons.

Many terrorist groups use the Internet for recruitment, propaganda and communication purposes. They may also conduct cyber-attacks against their enemies.

Some countries have started to investigate the use of the Internet to cause damage to the infrastructure of other countries. Targets would typically involve key businesses, the national power grid (for electricity supply), financial markets and government departments. The UK government has decided to set up a new office for cyber security. This department will monitor, analyse and counter any cyber-attacks.

It is interesting to note that as well as protecting against cyber warfare, many countries are investigating the potential of using cyber warfare itself should the need arise.

Many governments have turned to hackers who have the experience to know how to get past security methods and break into networks.

Cyber-attacks have already occurred. For example, there was an attack from China on the UK Foreign Office's computer.

Questions

1 a Explain what hacking is and why it is so important to keep hackers out of key networks. *(3 marks)*

   b Networks can be protected using firewalls.
      Explain how a firewall can be used to prevent unauthorized access.   *(2 marks)*

2 Give two examples of systems that could be hacked into and deliberately damaged as part of a cyber-attack.   *(2 marks)*

3 Some people think it is morally wrong to give good well-paid jobs to hackers who have deliberately broken the law.
   Say with reasons whether you agree or disagree with this.   *(2 marks)*

4 Terrorists use encryption to ensure the privacy of communication and to prevent being detected and caught.

   a Explain what encryption is and how it ensures the privacy of communication.   *(2 marks)*

   b Some countries are worried that encryption of data causes as many problems as it solves.
      Explain why a country might ban encryption.   *(2 marks)*

Case study 5

Wikipedia

Wikipedia was set up to empower and engage people around the world by collecting and offering free content which can be disseminated globally. It is a huge success story and has changed the way the Internet is used.

You will probably have already used Wikipedia but if not take a look at it now on:

www.wikipedia.com

Wikipedia is a charity, and unlike most other free providers of content, it does not contain adverts and therefore gets no money from these sources. Instead it relies mainly on asking you and me to donate money or on revenue from grants. The money it obtains is used to buy hardware and also for hosting the web site and bandwidth costs. People are not paid to add content – they do it for free!

Wikipedia is best described as an online encyclopaedia but it is different to other encyclopaedias in so much as it is made up from contributions by ordinary people.

You may think this is a bad thing. After all, what if the information is wrong? It is easy to put in bogus information or information which someone believes is true but is isn't. Luckily other people can add information which corrects the information that is already there.

The idea is that if enough people contribute, then the information is as good as that provided more traditionally.

Questions

1 Wikipedia is a good example of lots of people working collaboratively using ICT.

   a Explain what 'collaboratively' means. *(1 mark)*

   b Give one reason why some people like to contribute towards Wikipedia. *(1 mark)*

2 One commenter on Wikipedia said, 'there is plenty of bogus information on the Internet. What we don't want is non-experts making any old rubbish up on Wikipedia and then our children getting hold of it and believing it to be true'.
Give a reason why this is less likely to happen than the commenter thinks. *(2 marks)*

3 You have been asked to give a brief description of what Wikipedia is to someone who has little knowledge of ICT.
Describe Wikipedia in easy to understand non-technical language.
You should make at least three main points in your description. *(3 marks)*

ICT FOR IGCSE® TEACHER RESOURCE KIT

Case study 6

Phishing – tricking people to part with account information

Phishing is where fraudsters set up a fake website which looks the same as a bank website and then send out lots of emails to attract people to the site. When they go onto the fake site, they are asked to supply personal/financial details which can be used to steal their identity and money.

The name phishing arises because they are 'fishing' for personal information.

Shown below is an example of a 'phishing' email.

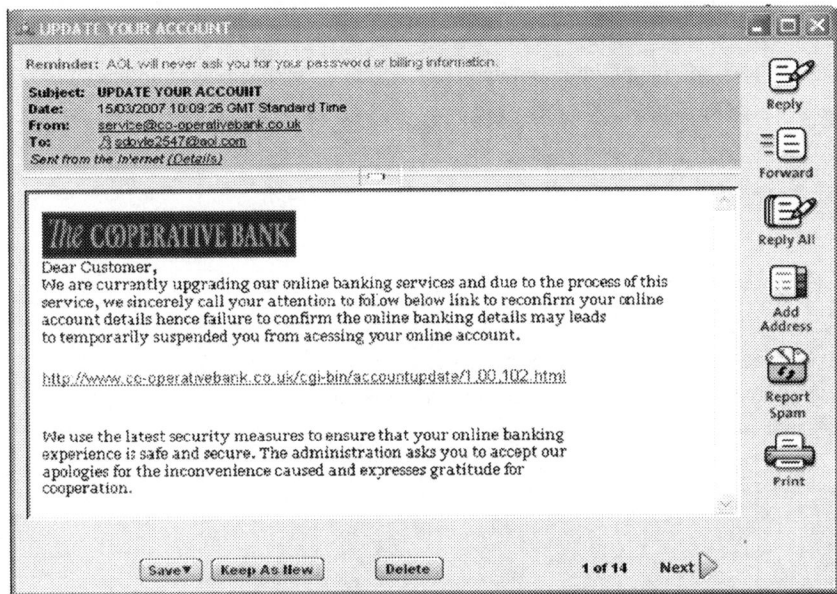

The phishing email looks genuine, but read it and see if there is anything that would make you suspicious?

When you click on the link in the email, you are directed to the following website:

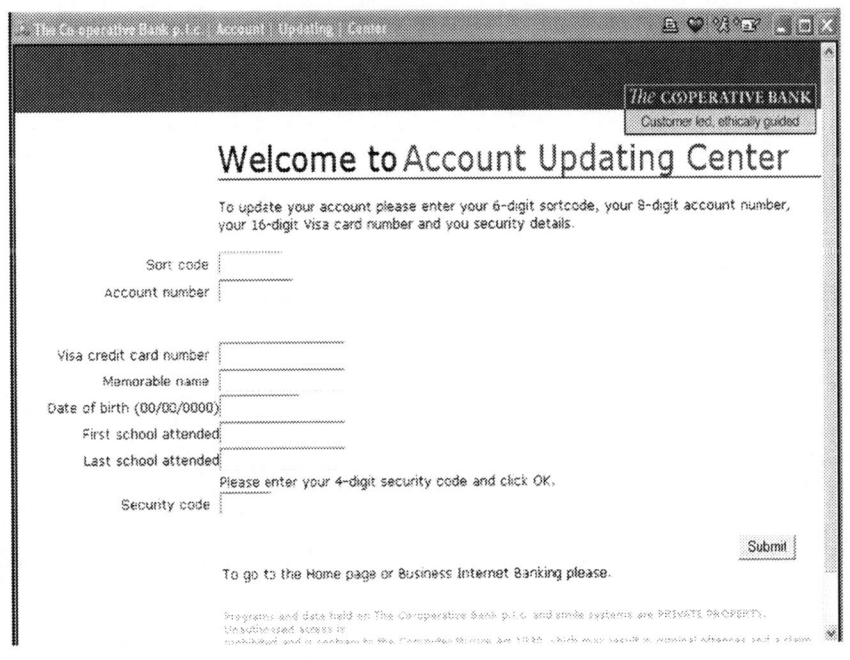

Case study 6 (continued)

If you were to supply this personal information, the fraudster would have enough detail to be able to steal your identity and buy goods and services using your credit card.

Notice that there is no indication that encryption is going to be used to scramble the information entered.

To combat phishing, banks now address you by name when sending you an email and also write down the last few numbers of your account number. Anyone sending you these fake emails would be unlikely to have these details normally, so you can be sure you are looking at an email from your bank.

Questions

1 As more people use the Internet for banking and buying goods and services online, there has been a huge increase in phishing.

Describe the meaning of the term phishing and give an example of how it works.   *(2 marks)*

2 When credit card or other personal/financial details are sent over the Internet, they are always encrypted before sending.

    a Explain what is meant by the term encryption.   *(2 marks)*

    b Give one reason why encryption is necessary.   *(2 marks)*

    c Many banks ask a security question before a transaction can be completed. Give an example of a security question.   *(1 mark)*

3 Banks and credit card companies are very worried about the increase in phishing.

Give two pieces of advice you would give to people who buy goods/services or who bank online, to help prevent them falling for these fake emails and sites.   *(2 marks)*

ICT FOR IGCSE® TEACHER RESOURCE KIT   © Oxford University Press 2012

Case study 7

ABS – a real-time system

Many cars are fitted with ABS (anti-lock braking system). ABS allows drivers to control their car when braking hard. Using ABS, when you brake hard, you will stop faster and in a more controlled manner than if you were driving the same car without ABS. ABS prevents wheels from locking and going into an uncontrollable skid. ABS works by detecting whether a particular wheel is about to lock and sending a message to the brake to relieve the pressure to stop the wheel locking. A real-time system is needed here because instant decisions need to be made based on the input data from the sensors. The processing therefore needs to be immediate.

Questions

1 Give one reason why batch processing would be unsuitable for a control system such as the ABS braking system used in some cars. *(2 marks)*

2 Real-time systems are used with control systems. Give one different example of a control system that would use real-time processing. *(1 mark)*

3 Many real-time systems make use of sensors. Give two reasons why this is so. *(2 marks)*

Case study 8

Using fingerprinting in schools

Many schools are now using fingerprinting methods to help with pupil registration.

One school has been using fingerprinting methods for a couple of years now. The system works by the pupils placing their finger on a scanner which is installed outside the classrooms. The scanner reads certain aspects of the print to identify the pupil and then records the attendance details on the computer.

The head teacher of the school has sung the praises of the system saying how it has helped reduce truancy because pupils now know that it can be immediately identified by the system. Teachers at the school have welcomed the system because it frees them from having to do this important but time-consuming task.

If a pupil fails to register at the start of the day, a text message can be sent to the parent's mobile phone alerting them of the non-attendance of their child. This makes it virtually impossible for a pupil not to attend school without their parents knowing.

Many pupils like the system because it gives them more time in the morning to chat with friends and find out what is going on in the school with their form teacher.

Some parents and pupils were initially worried that fingerprints were being routinely taken and stored by the school and that this was personal data which could be misused.

However, the company who supplied the system explained to parents that no full fingerprints are stored by the system. Instead the fingerprint is stored as a code and it is this code that is matched. They were reassured that a fingerprint cannot be re-created from this code and that it is only used by the school for identification purposes and not for some other sinister use.

Questions

1   Many schools use fingerprinting as a method for recording the presence of pupils at school.

  a   Fingerprinting is an example of a biometric input device.
      Explain briefly what this sentence means.   *(2 marks)*

  b   Give three advantages of using fingerprinting for registering attendance in schools.   *(3 marks)*

  c   Many parents may be worried that the system stores their child's fingerprints. Write a sentence to explain how you might address this worry.   *(2 marks)*

2   Describe one way in which the fingerprinting system helps prevent truancy in schools.   *(2 marks)*

3   Give one example of how this fingerprinting attendance system could possibly be misused.   *(2 marks)*

Case study 9

A fashion magazine making the most of communication

Bling, a new fashion magazine, brings the latest in fashion to its readers. There are two sides to the business: the editorial side and the business side.

The editorial side is where the freelance writers and journalists supply text for inclusion in the magazine, and the freelance photographers and graphic designers produce the photographs and artwork.

The business side is where the sales staff visit the newsagents and other retailers to take orders for the magazine. There are also other sales staff who sell advertising space in the magazine. There are also staff who deal with invoices and accounts and these are based at the head office in London.

The following communication services are used in the business:

▸▸ SMS/texting – staff spend time with customers or in meetings and do not want to take phone calls during this time so texting is a good way of contacting them.

▸▸ Fax – the editorial staff work together on the magazine. Faxing is good for sending copies of designs drawn on paper from one place to another.

▸▸ VoIP – phone calls are often made to other countries and the use of VoIP has reduced the costs of these calls along with calls made locally.

▸▸ Videoconferencing – meetings between the freelance staff and the staff employed at head office are difficult as the freelance staff live all over the country and a few of them live abroad. Traditional meetings take up too much time and mean people have to spend time away from their families. Videoconferencing enables staff to do all the things they do at meetings electronically.

▸▸ Email – this communication is used the most. Communication can be short and to the point. The freelance staff can attach files to the email. These attached files can contain text, photographs, graphics, etc.

▸▸ All people who do work for the magazine can access the company network. This can be done remotely (i.e. away from the head office) using the Internet. In order to access the network they need to enter their user-ID and a password. This allows sales staff to enter the orders placed by newsagents directly from their PDAs. The advantage in doing this is that it avoids paperwork, and fewer mistakes are made.

▸▸ All computers (including laptops and PDAs) have the following software installed to aid communication:

> ▸▸ Web browser software – so that searches of the Internet can be made for ideas for designs, looking at competitor magazines, looking at high street fashions, etc.

> ▸▸ Email software – so that a user can send and receive email, attach files, send emails to groups of co-workers, etc.

> ▸▸ Messaging software – so that VoIP phone calls can be made using the Internet. So that texts can be sent and received and so that instant messaging can be used.

Questions

1 a Give the name of the software used to view web pages.   (1 mark)

    b Give the name of the service which is most often used for sending and receiving digital messages from one computer to another using the Internet.   (1 mark)

2 When changing a password, explain why the user has to enter the password twice.   (2 marks)

3 Describe three advantages in using emails rather than telephone calls in order to give some important information.   (3 marks)

Case study 9 (continued)

4 Explain the difference between a text message and an IM (Instant Message). *(2 marks)*

5 Videoconferencing is used by many organizations to conduct face-to-face meetings at a distance.

   a Explain two advantages of videoconferencing. *(2 marks)*

   b Explain two disadvantages of videoconferencing. *(2 marks)*

6 When people are working remotely using ICT it can expose data to certain risks.

   a Give two methods by which you can ensure the security of the data held on the network. *(2 marks)*

   b There is a danger that when data is transferred using the Internet, it may be intercepted. Data is often encrypted when sent.
Explain what encryption means and why it helps secure data. *(2 marks)*

Case study 9 (continued)

Case study answers

Case study 1: Identity fraud

1 One mark for each of two pieces of advice such as:

Do not respond to emails asking for banking details/credit card details/passwords, etc.

Always check that a banking or other site has the correct URL before using it.

Use security/virus checking software to ensure that software which records your passwords is not present.

Check a site uses encryption before entering credit card/banking details.

Shred any paperwork before putting it in the rubbish.

2 One mark for the thing they can do and one mark for the consequences.

For example:

The thief can use the details online (1) for the purchase of goods or services (1).

They can steal the victim's identity (1) and open fraudulent accounts and loans (1).

Case study 2: Home copying

1 a One mark for each point to a maximum of two marks.

Taking a file from a larger computer

And transferring it over a network to your smaller computer

b One mark for a legal download such as:

Bought on a site on the Internet

Obtained from a site where the music has been donated freely by the artist

One mark for an illegal download such as:

An illegal file sharing site

2 a One mark for: They would lose money they would have obtained from the legal sales

b One mark for: They would not get any money/royalties for the illegal downloads

3 One mark each for two things which are copied illegally such as:

Large section of text

Photographs

Software

Human computer interfaces

Films/video

Case study 3: How using social networking sites might cause you health problems

1 One mark for: Repetitive strain injury.

2 One mark for each item to a maximum of two marks such as:

Meet new friends

Look at the profiles of other people

Search for people with similar interests to yourself

Look at other people's photographs

Send each other messages

Create a profile for yourself

Etc.

3 a Two marks for an answer similar to the following:

Working from home (1) by making use of ICT facilities and services (1)

b One mark for: Voice over Internet Protocol

c One mark for: Phone calls are much cheaper

d One mark for each point to a maximum of three marks.

Teleconferencing/videoconferencing

No time spent travelling to meetings

No costs such as travelling costs or hotel costs

No time spent away from home

Can work collaboratively without needing to be in the same place

4 One mark for each point to a maximum of two marks.

There are chemicals which fight disease (1) which are released when humans are in contact with each other (1).

These are not released during virtual meetings (1).

Case study 4: Cyber warfare

1 a One mark for each point to a maximum of three marks.

Unauthorized access to an ICT system

Usually but not necessarily using the Internet

Hackers can delete important data

This data can relate to terrorists, organised crime, etc.

It could be medical details for the whole country

This can easily cause loss of life

It could cause loss of infrastructure such as loss of air traffic control

b One mark for each point to a maximum of three marks.

Firewall is hardware, software or both

Used to prevent unauthorized access to a network

Blocks requests for certain data

Examines each incoming package of data

If package is not of a type allowed, it is rejected

2 One mark for each of two examples such as:

Nuclear power stations

MI5

Central medical databases

The Pentagon

Armed forces computer systems

NASA

Etc.

3 One mark for each point to a maximum of two marks.

Agree:

Hackers have a good understanding of methods used

They can point out vulnerabilities

They know other hackers and can 'grass' on them

Disagree

Rewarding them is morally wrong

It encourages hackers as they know they will get a well-paid job

Hacking could become a career pathway

You cannot pay criminals

4 a One mark for each point to a maximum of two marks.

Encryption scrambles the data into a code

You need a key to turn the data back to readable form

If a hacker intercepted the data, they would not be able to understand it

If the data was stolen (e.g. on a laptop) the data would be unreadable

Useful for sending banking details over the Internet

b One mark for each point to a maximum of two marks.

Encryption can be used by terrorists or criminals

It enables them to have conversations in private

Prevents surveillance from taking place

Makes it harder for security services to collect evidence

Harder to gain prosecutions

Case study 5: Wikipedia

1 a One mark for one of the following:

Actively working together

More than one person working on the same project

b One mark for one of the following:

They find it interesting

It is a hobby

They like to help everyone using their specialist knowledge

They like to build up their knowledge of a subject

2 One mark each for two relevant points such as:

Others can add information which corrects what has been added

There are lots of viewers so mistakes are quickly spotted

3 One mark for each point to a maximum of three:

It is an online encyclopaedia

Created collaboratively/by lots of people

Uses money from donations to keep it running

People add their own content

Others can make corrections

Etc.

Case study 6: Phishing – tricking people to part with account information

1 One mark for definition and one mark for suitable example.

Phishing means sending fake emails to lots of different people in the hope that some of them might divulge credit card details and passwords. These details could then be used to commit a range of frauds such as buying goods or services using the details or even taking out loans by forging a person's identity.

2 a One mark for mentioning 'coding' and other mark for 'unable to read encrypted data' or similar.

Encryption means coding data so that even if it were intercepted, the person would be unable to read or understand the encrypted data.

b Two marks for answer similar to the following:

To ensure the privacy and the security of credit card and bank account details when ordering goods or services over the Internet or performing online banking.

c One mark for any security question such as:

Mother's maiden name

Name of first school attended, etc.

3 Two marks for any advice similar to two of the following:

Never give details of account numbers, credit card numbers, expiry dates, etc., to anyone.

Watch out for fake emails with spelling mistakes, grammatical errors, etc.

Be very careful when entering passwords, etc., into sites as they may not be genuine sites.

Case study 7: ABS – a real time system

1 Two marks for an answer similar to:

Batch processing collects data over time and then processes it (1). ABS processes data in real time (1).

2 One mark for a different example of a control system such as:

Central heating system to control the temperature in a room

Process control system such as making chemicals

3 Two marks for two points:

Data is read from sensors automatically (1) and fed to the computer for processing (1). An immediate decision based on the data can be made and this determines the output (1).

Case study 8: Using fingerprinting in schools

1 a Any two points (one mark each) similar to:

Uses properties of the human body (1) which are unique for a particular person (1) such as fingerprints or pattern on retina (1) to uniquely identify that person (1)

b Any three from the following list (one mark each):

Scanning and recognition are performed quickly

Pupils cannot register for others

Because the system is so quick it means pupils can be registered for each lesson

Improves attendance rates as system automatically sends texts about non-attendance to parents

Frees teachers from taking registers

Give pupils more responsibility for their attendance

c Two marks for two points similar to the following:

Fingerprint images are not stored

Only certain points of the image are stored

The pattern of the points is coded and stored

Manufacturers say that fingerprints cannot be re-created from the stored code

2 One mark for each point to a max of two marks for:

System records pupil attendance in almost real time (1). Parents can be immediately informed if their child is not in school (1) using a text message which the system sends automatically (1) – acts as a deterrent against truancy (1).

3 Two marks for two valid points:

All children could be routinely scanned for fingerprints (1), meaning the government could eventually have a database of everyone's fingerprints (1), which would erode privacy (1) but could be used by the police to solve crimes (1).

Case study 9: A fashion magazine making the most of communication

1 a One mark for web browser software

b One mark for email software

2 One mark for each point to a maximum of two marks.

To ensure they have typed in the password they meant to type in (1) as they are unlikely to make the same mistake twice (1)

As a method of verification (1) to ensure that the correct password has been typed (1)

3 One mark for each of three advantages such as:

They can be printed out

They can be forwarded easily to others

They are received almost instantly

They can be saved for future reference

People can receive them from lots of different devices (mobile phones, PDAs, etc.)

4 One mark for an incomplete explanation of the difference and two marks for a more complete explanation.

Text messages are sent using a service called SMS

IMs are sent using the Internet

You can have conversations in real time using IMs

5 a One mark for each of two advantages such as:

No time is wasted travelling to meetings

It is greener because fewer journeys are made

Meetings can be organized and held at the last minute

People do not have to spend time away from their families

b One mark for each of two disadvantages such as:

Some people like to travel to meetings

You cannot handle a real product virtually

The social interaction with real people is important to people who work remotely

6 a One mark each for two methods such as:

Ensure regular backups are kept

Ensure a firewall is installed to protect against hackers

Install the latest virus scanning software and keep it up-to-date

Ensure the computer is protected by passwords

Encrypt any personal data stored

b One mark each for two points made similar to the following:

It scrambles the data before being transferred

So that if it is intercepted, the data cannot be understood

Exam support

Here are some examination style questions showing how a student has answered the question and what is wrong with their answers. Also included is a model answer.

Topic 1

Types and components of computer systems

WORKED EXAMPLE

Graphical user interfaces (GUIs) are a feature of the operating system on most computers.

a Explain why a computer needs a user interface. *(2 marks)*

b Give **one** input device, other than a keyboard, that can be used with a graphical user interface. *(1 mark)*

c Give **four** features of a graphical user interface. *(4 marks)*

d **i** Give **one** other type of user interface. *(1 mark)*

  ii Give **two** benefits to an inexperienced user offered by a graphical user interface compared with this type of interface. *(2 marks)*

Student answer 1

a The user interface provides an interface between the computer and the user.

  It allows the user to use the computer.

b Mouse

c Pull-down menus

  Windows

  Icons

  Menus

d **i** Menu driven interface

  ii Menus only allow a few things to be done whereas with a GUI you can have lots of icons to click on

Comment

a This is a typical answer given by students who do not know the answer. They use the words in the question and put these in the answer. Neither of these answers is awarded a mark.

b This is a correct piece of hardware so one mark is awarded.

c Pull-down menus and menus are not distinctly different so only one mark can be given rather than two. The other answers are correct. Three marks are given.

d **i** This is a correct type of interface so one mark is given.

  ii This is only one benefit so only one mark is awarded. Students must always check that they have given the correct number of answers.

(6 marks out of 10)

ICT FOR IGCSE® TEACHER RESOURCE KIT   © Oxford University Press 2012

Student answer 2

a The user interface is the point where the user and the computer meet. The user interface provides a way of the user interacting with the computer. For example, they can issue commands by clicking on menu items and icons.

b Touch screen

c Windows

Icons

Pointers

Menus

d i Windows

ii The icons in a GUI have small pictures that help a user understand what they do. Graphical user interfaces are almost the norm so once a user has learnt one type of interface they will be able to use others easily.

Comment

a There are three valid points made here so the maximum of two marks is given here.

b A touch screen can be considered to be an input device (and also an output device) and they have become increasingly popular so this is a valid answer and one mark is awarded.

c Four correct features of a GUI have been given, so four marks are awarded.

d i Never give a brand name unless the question specifically asks for it. This means that Windows is not an acceptable answer so no marks for this answer.

ii There are two points made here and the argument about the GUI in the last point could be put forward about a menu driven interface. In this case, the examiner has used their discretion and has given this student both the marks.

(9 marks out of 10)

Answers

a One mark for each of the following points to a maximum of two marks:

▸▸ Allows a user to communicate with the computer

▸▸ The way the computer interacts with the user

▸▸ It allows the user to make selections

▸▸ It provides a dialogue between the computer and the user

b One mark for one of the following:

▸▸ Mouse

▸▸ Touch pad

▸▸ Tracker ball

▸▸ Touch screen

▸▸ Etc.

c Any four from the following (one mark each):

▸▸ Windows

▶▶ Icons

▶▶ Menus/Pull-down menus

▶▶ Pointers

▶▶ Online help/Office assistants

d **i** One mark for one of the following:

▶▶ Menu driven interface

▶▶ Command line interface

▶▶ Voice driven interface/interface making use of voice recognition

ii One mark each for two benefits such as:

▶▶ Standard look and feel

▶▶ Interfaces are similar so they are easier to learn and skills can be transferred

▶▶ More intuitive (users can usually figure out what they have to do)

▶▶ Use of icons with pictures makes it easy for users to work out what each button does

ICT FOR IGCSE® TEACHER RESOURCE KIT   © Oxford University Press 2012

Topic 2

Input and output devices

WORKED EXAMPLE

Web cams can take live video which can be transferred using the Internet to a computer in the home.

a Tick the **three** applications that are possible using a web cam.   *(3 marks)*

	Tick **three** boxes
Watching the evolution of dinosaurs	
A parent checking up on their children in a nursery when they are at work	
Looking at live video of an erupting volcano in a geography lesson	
Watching a movie star constantly wherever they go	
Watching the space shuttle taking off as it happens	

b Give **two** advantages of using a web cam.   *(2 marks)*

c Give **two** disadvantages of using a web cam.   *(2 marks)*

Student answer 1

a

	Tick **three** boxes
Watching the evolution of dinosaurs	√
A parent checking up on their children in a nursery when they are at work	
Looking at live video of an erupting volcano in a geography lesson	
Watching a movie star constantly wherever they go	√
Watching the space shuttle taking off as it happens	√

b You can use it to spy on other people

They are very cheap to buy and many computers have them built into the screen

c They do not produce a very good image

You cannot store the image produced

Comment

a Web cams produce live images so you obviously cannot watch the evolution of dinosaurs.

Watching a movie star wherever they go would require a web cam to be present all the time. Clearly this is false.

The last tick is in the correct box.

b The first answer is a bit vague and needed further amplification to get the mark. The second answer is ok and gains a mark.

c The first answer is correct and gains a mark.

It is possible to save an image produced by a web cam and this is how they are used for security purposes.

(3 marks out of 7)

Student answer 2

a

	Tick **three** boxes
Watching the evolution of dinosaurs	
A parent checking up on their children in a nursery when they are at work	√
Looking at live video of an erupting volcano in a geography lesson	√
Watching a movie star constantly wherever they go	
Watching the space shuttle taking off as it happens	√

b You can look at famous sites throughout the world using live or almost live pictures

They can be used for surveillance by the police and MI5 as they are extremely small

c They can be used to make secret films of people without their knowledge which is morally wrong

Web cams can encourage online flirting with people who are married which could destroy a marriage

Comment

a All the ticks are in the correct places so all three marks are given here.

b Both of these are advantages of web cams, so full marks for this part.

c Both of these answers are valid and so full marks are awarded.

(7 marks out of 7)

Answers

a One mark for each correctly placed tick:

	Tick **three** boxes
Watching the evolution of dinosaurs	
A parent checking up on their children in a nursery when they are at work	√
Looking at live video of an erupting volcano in a geography lesson	√
Watching a movie star constantly wherever they go	
Watching the space shuttle taking off as it happens	√

b One mark for each of two advantages such as:

They can record criminals and be used as evidence

You can see what the weather is like in a resort you are soon to visit

They are very cheap to buy

You can chat with people and see them at the same time

They are small and so can be hidden easily so people do not know you are looking at them

Web cams means that you can have a simple meeting without the need to travel

People can view things in distant places that it would be hard for them to visit in person

c One mark for each of two disadvantages such as:

The images from web cams are often poor quality

It can make it easy for others to spy on you without you knowing

It can invade people's privacy

Topic 3

Storage devices and media

WORKED EXAMPLE

A presentation that contains multimedia features such as images, sound and video is to be transferred between computers.

a Give the names of **two** storage devices that can be used to store the files and explain why they are suitable for this application. *(4 marks)*

b All storage devices and media have disadvantages. For each storage device/media you have named in (a) state **two** disadvantages. *(2 marks)*

Student answer 1

a CD – because lots of different files can be stored and all computers come with a CD drive

DVD – because the storage capacity is high and they work with all computers

b CD – you cannot store data on both side of the disk

DVD – the surface of this disk can easily be damaged which causes them not to work

Comment

a Just stating either CD or DVD will not gain marks. As the presentation has been created on one computer and needs to be transferred to a different computer, there needs to be a write facility so it is necessary to give the names DVD RW or CD RW.

In other questions where the write facility is not needed, the proper terms DVD ROM or CD ROM should be used rather than CD or DVD.

No marks for part (a)

b The lack of storage on both sides could (loosely) be considered as a limitation. The problem here is that the top surface tends to get scratched and also where would you put the label? Optical media is easily damaged so part (b) is an acceptable answer.

(2 marks out of 6)

Student answer 2

a CD RW – because the data can be recorded onto a CD RW disk that has a high storage capacity that is ideal for all the multimedia files. Also all computers have a drive that is capable of reading the data off the disk.

Flash drive – the drive can be used just like another drive and has a high enough capacity to hold all the files needed and it is easy to transport being small in size and light.

b CD RW – you have to take care when handling them as it is very easy to scratch the disk surface and prevent the CD RW from being able to transfer data.

Flash drive — the access time is lower than that for an internal magnetic hard drive which means the data takes longer to load.

Comment

a The student has identified suitable storage devices/media and has clearly related their reasons to the transfer of multimedia files for a presentation. This part gains full marks.

b Two disadvantages of each storage media/device have been identified so full marks for this.

(6 marks out of 6)

Answers

a One mark for each device and one mark for the reason x 2.

Pen drive – small size means easily transferred from one computer to another

Pen drive – can be used by all computers as it simply plugs into the USB port/socket

Pen drive – can get cheap storage capacity which is enough for large music, animation, image files needed for a multimedia presentation

CD RW – has a large storage capacity, which is needed because multimedia files are usually large

CD RW – small in size which means they are easily transferred between computers

CD RW – can be read by any computer with a CD drive or a DVD drive

b One mark for each disadvantage. Note the disadvantages must refer to the named storage devices in part (a).

CD RW – easily scratched which causes read problems

CD RW – limited amount of storage capacity

Pen drive – low access speed/transfer rate compared to a magnetic hard drive

Pen drive – easily bent and broken when in the USB port

Pen drive – often left in the machine by mistake and lost

Topic 4

Computer networks

WORKED EXAMPLE

A small lawyers' office has ten stand-alone computers. They have been told that it is much more effective if all the computers are formed into a network.

State **three** benefits that the organization would gain from networking their computers together. *(6 marks)*

Student answer 1

They would be able to access the Internet

They would be able to send email to each other without using the Internet, which would be cheaper

They could all use the same data

Comment

The first sentence is not strictly true. Stand-alone computers can of course access the Internet. What they probably meant to say is that by networking the computers together they could all share a single Internet connection.

The examiner cannot read their mind and can only mark what appears, so this sentence is not worthy of a mark.

The second sentence is true and well explained because they could still send email to each other using the Internet but this can compromise the security of the data, so organizations like to send email internally without using the Internet.

The last sentence is worth one mark.

The student should have looked at the mark scheme and realized that there are two marks for each benefit. So a brief benefit for one mark and further explanation of the benefit or an example should have been included for each.

(2 marks out of 6)

Student answer 2

Using a network they are able to share resources such as printers and scanners. This means that they need only buy one of each rather than one for each computer, which will be much cheaper.

Any computer will be able to access files stored on the server. This means it will not be necessary for data to be copied so that it can be transferred between the computers.

All the computers will be able to share a single Internet connection. This will be cheaper as all they need to buy is a router and they can then only pay for a single fast connection.

Comment

This is a very well-structured and thought out answer. Notice the way they have sectioned their answer. The first sentence introduces the benefit and then extra sentences add further explanation.

This good examination technique has helped this student gain all the marks for this question.

(6 marks out of 6)

Answers

One mark each for a statement of the benefit and one mark for an explanation of the benefit x 3:

▶▶ Ability to share files (1) – no need to make copies of files as all the files can be accessed by all the computers on the network if needed (1).

▶▶ Ability to share hardware resources (1) – no need to have a printer for each computer as any hardware device (e.g., printer, scanner, plotter, etc.) can be shared (1).

▶▶ Ability to share software (1) – software can be shared, meaning that everyone will be using the same version. Maintaining software by keeping it up-to-date is made much easier (1).

▶▶ Lower software costs (1) – it is cheaper to buy one network version with a licence for so many users compared to buying individual copies for each computer (1).

▶▶ Improved security (1) – it is easier for network managers to control access to the Internet (1).

▶▶ Can share an Internet connection (1) – one connection can allow all users access (1).

▶▶ Easier to back up files (1) – backing up is performed by the network manager rather than the individual users, which means backing up is taken seriously and users are less likely to lose data (1).

▶▶ Improved communication (1) – networks have email facilities, which will improve communication between workers (1).

▶▶ Central maintenance and support (1) – new upgrades to software need only to be added to the server and not to each computer (1).

Topic 5

Data types

WORKED EXAMPLE

The manager of a tool hire company wishes to use a relational database to help keep track of the business. The databases stores the data in three tables, called: Tools, Customers and Rentals.

a Explain what a relational database is and what its main features are.   *(5 marks)*

b What are the main advantages to this manager in storing the data in a relational database rather than a flat-file database?   *(3 marks)*

Student answer 1

a A relational database is a database that has relationships between it. The relationships mean that you can get all the data out of the database in whatever order you want. Relational databases are proper databases and are good for businesses that use them a lot.

b The manager will be able to access the data from lots of different places.

   To put the data into the relational database requires less typing as you only need to put the data in one file.

   The manager will be able to find out information such as which customer has which tool.

Comment

a The first sentence could be thought up by anyone using the term 'relational database' so it gets no marks. To obtain the marks, they would need to mention that the relationships are links formed between tables.

   The other sentences are vague statements and this student obviously knows little about these databases. No marks are awarded for this part of the answer.

b In the first sentence the student looks as though they are getting mixed up with distributed databases. The second sentence is a main advantage in using relational databases and therefore gets one mark. The third sentence is not specific and is awarded no marks.

(1 mark out of 8)

Student answer 2

a A relational database consists of a collection of data organized into different tables with each table containing a set of data that is relevant to the organization. Three tables would be used here; a customer table, a tool table and a rentals table.

   The data is put into the separate tables but the tables are linked together so it is possible to combine the information from data in all the tables.

---

b He won't have to type as much in as there is not as much duplication of data as there would be with a flat file.

If a customer changed their address then with a flat file the manager would have to change the address in each current record where a piece of equipment has been hired. This means that if a customer has hired five different pieces of equipment the address would need changing five times.

Comment

a There are three separate points made here so three marks.

b This student has mentioned duplication of data and easier updating process and has explained each of these well. Two marks are given here.

(5 marks out of 8)

Answers

a One mark each for five features of a relational database.

- ▶▶ Note they must be features and not advantages.
- ▶▶ Databases that do not store all the data in a single table.
- ▶▶ They use several tables.
- ▶▶ Tables are linked together (or mention of relationships).
- ▶▶ Data in one table can be combined with data in any of the other tables.

b One mark each for three distinctly different advantages that must be relevant to this application.

- ▶▶ Full customer details do not need to be entered when a customer who has rented before, rents again.
- ▶▶ If a mail shot needs to go out to customers, the manager will not need to go through all the orders extracting names and addresses as you can use the Customer table.
- ▶▶ An update is easier to make as the manager will only need to alter the data the once in one of the tables.
- ▶▶ The data is stored more efficiently so it will be faster to do searches and sorts.
- ▶▶ There will be fewer data errors since the data is only entered once, which means the manager can rely on the information produced.

Topic 6

The effects of using ICT

WORKED EXAMPLE

Computer viruses are a threat to computer systems.

a Explain what is meant by a computer virus. *(2 marks)*

b Give **one** thing that a computer virus might do on a computer system. *(1 mark)*

c Give **one** way of preventing computer viruses entering a system. *(1 mark)*

Student answer 1

a A program that does damage

b Destroy the computer

c Use McAfee to stop viruses getting into your computer

Comment

a This is a bit vague because it is not specific about what it does damage to. Only one mark is given for this answer.

b This is a typical answer given by a weak pupil. Viruses can be removed and therefore cannot be said to 'destroy' the computer. No marks for this.

c Brand names should never be given. So instead of McAfee they should have said 'anti-virus software'. No marks are given for this answer.

(1 mark out of 4)

Student answer 2

a A mischievous program that copies itself onto your computer and does harm by messing up settings or deleting data

b It can start to make your computer run slow and can also cause it to crash unexpectedly

c Use anti-virus software to scan for viruses and remove them if they are found

Comment

a A good answer which makes it clear that it is a program that copies itself so this answer is worth two marks.

b Again another good answer which gains one mark.

c This answer is correct and gains one mark.

(4 marks out of 4)

Answers

a Two marks allocated in the following way:

Program that copies itself automatically (1) and causes damage to data or causes the computer to run slowly (1)

b One mark for an answer such as:

Can erase files which means the operating system software cannot be loaded

Can cause the deletion of data

Can cause the computer to crash

Can cause the changing of settings, which causes annoyance to the user

Can copy passwords and usernames and transmit these to another person

c One mark for one of the following:

Don't open file attachments unless you know who they are from

Install anti-virus software

Keep anti-virus software up-to-date

Don't download files from unknown sources

Topic 7

The ways in which ICT is used

WORKED EXAMPLE 1

1   A cutter in a clothing manufacturing company is controlled by a computer. The cutter
    is used to cut various patterns in cloth automatically using the following instructions.

START	means start program
CUTTER UP	means raise the cutter up
CUTTER DOWN	means lower the cutter down
FORWARD 10	means forward 10
BACKWARD 5	means backward 5
RIGHT 90	means right turn 90 degrees
LEFT 45	means left turn 45 degrees
CLEAR SCREEN	means clear screen
END	means end program

The cutter always starts with the cutter up so that it does not start cutting. When the
END command is used the cutter will automatically return to its starting position.

a   Write a program using instructions similar to the above that will cut out the shape
    shown here:

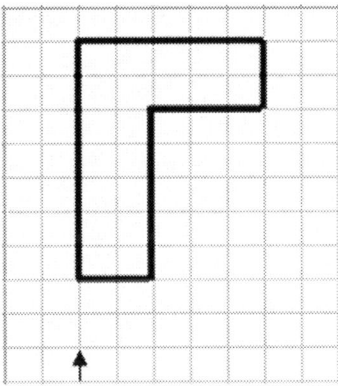

Starting position is at the tip of the arrow   *(3 marks)*

b   On the blank grid drawn below draw the shape that the cutter will cut out when
    carrying out the following program.

START

FORWARD 6

CUTTER DOWN

FORWARD 3

RIGHT 90

FORWARD 7

RIGHT 90

FORWARD 7

RIGHT 90

FORWARD 2

RIGHT 90

FORWARD 4

LEFT 90

FORWARD 5

CUTTER UP

END

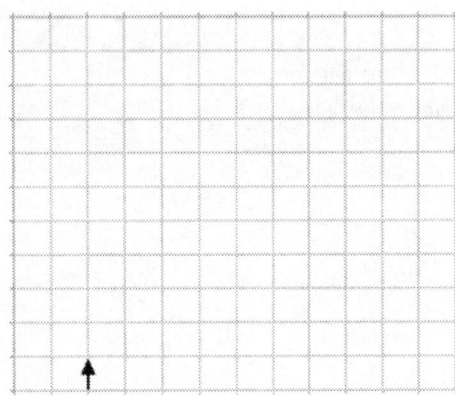

(2 marks)

c   Give **two** reasons why it would be difficult for the cutter to cut out a complex shape
using only those commands given above. (2 marks)

Student answer 1

1 a

FORWARD 7

RIGHT 90

FORWARD 5

RIGHT 90

FORWARD 2

RIGHT 90

FORWARD 3

LEFT 90

FORWARD 5

RIGHT 90

FORWARD 2

END

b

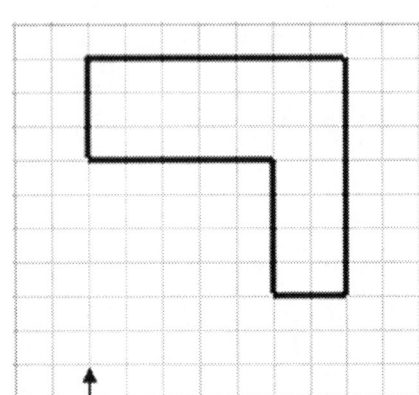

c   You can't go diagonally because the diagonal distances are
more than one square

You can only go in straight lines

Comment

1 a There is no start command instructing the computer to start obeying the set of instructions. Also the student has started from where the shape starts and not from where the tip of the arrow is. There is also no instruction CD telling the cutter to go down and start cutting. The middle section of commands is correct but the student has failed to raise the cutter before the END command.

Only one mark is given for the middle section of correct commands.

b The student has drawn the correct shape for the instructions so full marks (i.e. 2 marks) are given.

c These are both valid reasons so two marks here.

(5 marks out of 7)

Student answer 2

1 a FORWARD 2
    CUTTER DOWN
    RIGHT 90
    FORWARD 2
    LEFTT 90
    FORWARD 5
    RIGHT 90
    FORWARD 3
    LEFT 90
    FORWARD 2
    LEFT 90
    FORWARD 5
    LEFT 90
    FORWARD 7
    CUTTER UP
    END

b

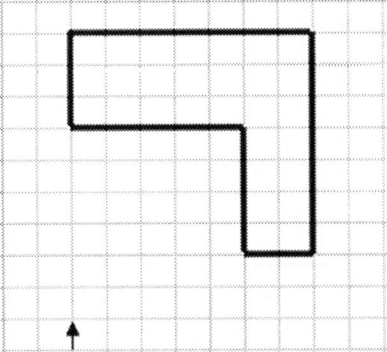

c You cannot give the instructions for curves.

Although you can move through angles it would be hard to know what distances to choose.

Comment

1 a Most people would take a clockwise path around the shape but this student has decided to go anticlockwise. This is perfectly OK and these instructions will correctly cut the shape so three marks are given.

b The shape drawn on the gird is correct, so a full two marks here.

c Both reasons are correct so two marks are awarded.

(7 marks out of 7)

Answers

a One mark for all Box 1 steps correct

One mark for all Box 2 steps correct

One mark for all Box 3 steps correct

This is only one of the many possible answers. There is another correct answer given by a student in Student answer 2.

```
START
FORWARD 2
CUTTER DOWN
FORWARD 7
RIGHT 90
FORWARD 5
```

```
RIGHT 90
FORWARD 2
RIGHT 90
FORWARD 3
LEFTT 90
FORWARD 5
```

```
RIGHT 90
FORWARD 2
CUTTER UP
END
```

b

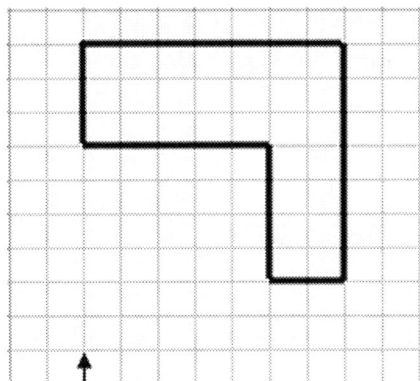

One mark for this section correctly drawn

START

FORWARD 6

CUTTER DOWN

FORWARD 3

RIGHT 90

FORWARD 7

RIGHT 90

One mark for this section correctly drawn

FORWARD 7

RIGHT 90

FORWARD 2

RIGHTT 90

FORWARD 4

LEFT 90

FORWARD 5

CUTTER UP

c One mark for each one to a maximum of two marks.

The cutter can only travel in straight lines

You cannot cut a smooth curve

The diagonal distances are not known so it is hard to move the cutter accurately through an angle

WORKED EXAMPLE 2

2 a Define what is meant by a robot. *(2 marks)*

   b Robots are used in industry for a variety of tasks.

     Give **two** tasks that robots are often used for in industry. *(2 marks)*

   c Give **three** advantages in using robots in industry. *(3 marks)*

Student answer 1

2 a A robot is a device like a human which walks around and talks

b For spraying cars

For welding panels on cars

c You do not need to pay them so they are cheaper

They can do the job better than a person because they do not have off days

They work hard all the time not like humans who can be lazy

Comment

2 a This sounds more like the type of robot seen on Star Wars or in children toys. Students are best advised to remember definitions of key words like the word robot.

No marks are given for this answer.

b The student should have given more detail and mentioned 'for spraying cars with paint'. However, they were not penalized for this.

Both of the answers here were awarded a mark.

c All the answers here are correct so this part gains full marks.

(5 marks out of 7)

Student answer 2

2 a It is a device that can be programmed to do a particular task such as assemble parts of a car engine. If you want the robot to do a different task, then you have to reprogram it

For welding the spouts on electric kettles

For packing goods in boxes ready to be sent to customers

Robots can work continuously for long periods

The robots can work 24 hours a day 365 days per year

Once you have paid for them, the costs to keep them working is very low compared to employing staff

Comment

2 a This is a good answer that tells the examiner that robots can be programmed and that they are capable of being reprogrammed. The fact that robots can be reprogrammed makes them robots and not simply automatic devices such as a washing machine. Full marks are given for this answer.

b Both are jobs performed by robots so full marks are given again.

c The first two points made are almost the same so only one mark is given. It is always worth checking that your answers are distinctly different.

The second point is worth a mark.

(6 marks out of 7)

ICT FOR IGCSE® TEACHER RESOURCE KIT

Answers

2 **a** One mark for each of two points such as:

A machine that can be programmed

To perform a series of actions

And is capable of being reprogrammed to carry out different actions or a different task

b One mark for each task to a maximum of two marks.

Paint spraying

Welding panels

Assembling components

Moving goods around a factory

c One mark for each advantage to a maximum of three marks.

Robots do not get tired or distracted

Robots do not have to be paid

They are capable of working 24/7

They can work in dangerous conditions

They are consistent and produce high quality work

They can create some new jobs such as the people who maintain or program them

WORKED EXAMPLE 3

3 Medical expert systems are used by doctors.

    a Describe the **three** main parts of every expert system.   *(3 marks)*

    b Describe, using examples, **two** advantages of using an expert system in medicine.   *(2 marks)*

Student answer 1

3 **a** Database

    Inference engine

    GUI

 b It enables an inexperienced doctor to do the job of a consultant

    It saves time

Comment

3 **a** Database is not correct. The correct answer is 'knowledge base' which consists of factual knowledge and information about making good judgements.

GUI (graphical user interface) is one type of interface that can be used as the interface between the user and the system. However, the correct answer is 'user interface' so this mark would not be given.

One mark for the correct answer 'Inference engine'.

 b There is no way the inexperienced doctor becomes a consultant through using an expert system. Expert systems are only used in a small area of medicine usually to aid diagnosis. 'Saving time' on its own gains no marks. Here the students should have said in what way the system saves time.

(1 mark out of 5)

Student answer 2

3 a Knowledge base

Inference or reasoning engine

User interface

b They can base their diagnosis on a lot more facts than a human can

They will go through steps that a human expert may forget to take to arrive at a more accurate diagnosis

Comment

3 a All correct answers here. Both the answers 'Inference or reasoning engine' are correct.

b Both of these answers are distinctly different and correct so full marks for this part.

(5 marks out of 5)

Answers

3 a One mark each to a maximum of three for:

Knowledge base

Inference engine

User interface

b One mark each to a maximum of two marks for:

Leaves doctors/specialists more time to concentrate on serious cases

The knowledge base can be kept more up-to-date.

Ordinary doctors can use the system to make an expert diagnosis without needing to contact a specialist

There is faster diagnosis for patients so patients get better quicker

It is cheaper to use the expert system than train doctors in the specialist area

A human may forget to consider a certain fact but the expert system will consider all the facts to arrive at a correct diagnosis

WORKED EXAMPLE 4

4 Many people now choose to bank online because of the time savings it offers. They do not have to travel to the bank and then probably queue up.

There are other advantages of online banking. Discuss the other advantages and possible disadvantages to the bank customer. *(6 marks)*

Student answer 1

Quicker – it is much quicker to use online banking

Easier – you can sit at home and do it

Safer – you can pay money without the need to draw cash out to pay bills

The worry of hackers accessing your bank account may make it not worth your while having an online account

Comment

4 In the question the student was asked to 'discuss' the advantages and disadvantages. This means that they are expected to answer in sentences and not simply give a list of points.

In addition to this, the student has fallen into the trap of using the words 'Quicker' and 'Easier' without saying why.

There are no marks for the first three points.

The last point is made in a sentence and this is a valid disadvantage.

(1 mark out of 6)

Student answer 2

4 Online accounts often give the best rates of interest because the banks operating costs are lower than high street banks.

Customers do not have to waste time travelling to banks and queuing up to do simple transactions that they could do from home.

Customers no longer have to store their own paper bank statements as they can all be viewed online.

Goods are often bought by mail order or over the Internet.

It is possible to pay by transferring money to another person's account using online banking which saves having to write a cheque or reveal credit card details.

Some customers will be worried about unauthorized access to their online account by hackers who could commit fraud.

Comment

4 This student has correctly given their answers in proper sentences and they have discussed more than four correct advantages/disadvantages in detail. The explanations given were very clear.

(6 marks out of 6)

Answers

4 Candidates may discuss a range of the following:

Advantages

A customer can move money between current and savings accounts quickly in order to take advantage of better rates of interest

Customers can check all their statements online rather than have to store paper statements

Online accounts frequently have better rates of interest

You can pay bills or put money directly into another account from your home

Online accounts offer 24/7 access so you can bank outside normal banking hours

There is no paperwork with account numbers on to discard so there is reduced risk of identity theft

You can apply for loans, overdrafts and credit cards without having to visit a bank

It allows you to pay for goods and services without using cash or cheques, which is easier

Disadvantages

Online bank accounts could be hacked into and your money stolen

You cannot get cash so you still need to visit a cash machine

Older people may prefer the personal service offered by a conventional bank

ICT FOR IGCSE® TEACHER RESOURCE KIT © Oxford University Press 2012

Topic 8

Systems analysis and design

WORKED EXAMPLE 1

When a new system is produced it should be thoroughly tested. A testing plan is produced that uses normal, extreme and abnormal data. This test plan is carried out during the development and testing stage.

a Give **one** reason why a system should be tested. *(1 mark)*

b A test plan is created in the development and testing stage of the systems life cycle.

   Explain what is meant by a test plan. *(1 mark)*

c Explain what is meant by each of the following:

   i   Normal data *(1 mark)*

   ii Extreme data *(1 mark)*

   iii Abnormal data *(1 mark)*

Student answer 1

a To make sure it works

b It is a plan that tests all the parts of the system

c i This is just ordinary data that you input. It is not too big or small and will not be rejected by the system

   ii This is data that is too big or small and should be rejected by the system

   iii This is data that is just on the border of what is acceptable

Comment

a This is far too vague for a mark. Most systems will 'probably work' but a user wants a system to work without any errors. No marks for this answer.

b This is a typical answer where the student simply gives an answer based on what is in the question. No marks here.

c i This is just about OK for a mark.

   ii This is an incorrect definition so no mark here.

   iii The student is getting mixed up here with extreme data. No marks for this answer.

(1 mark out of 5)

Student answer 2

a To make sure that the system works as expected by performing a number of tests.

b The test plan includes lists of which tests are to be carried out with data to test and what should happen to the data when it is entered.

c i This is data that should be accepted by the system for processing.

---

ii This is data that is on the borderline of what is acceptable.

iii This is data that is completely incorrect and should be rejected by the system.

Comment

a This is a good answer and gains one mark.

b This is a very good description of a test plan and gains one mark.

c i This is an acceptable answer so one mark is awarded.

ii This is a good answer so one mark.

iii Another good answer so one mark.

(5 marks out of 5)

Answers

a One mark for an answer such as:

Testing involves performing a series of checks to ensure that the system works as expected.

b One mark for an answer such as:

A detailed list of checks to be performed to test the system.

c i One mark for answer similar to the following:

This is data that will pass all the validation rules and will be accepted for processing.

Alternatively an example can be given:

Mark greater than or equal to 0 and also less than or equal to 100 so a typical piece of data would lie in this range.

ii One mark for an answer similar to the following:

It is a piece of data on the borderline of what is accepted.

Or a clear example such as:

For example, if an exam mark can be from 0 to 100 then 0 and 100 are examples of extreme data.

iii One mark for an answer similar to the following:

Data that is outside the validation checks and should be rejected by the system.

WORKED EXAMPLE 2

2 A school keeps details of all its students on a computer. Part of the data is shown below. The data is structured in fields, records and files.

Student_Number	Surname	Forename	Date of birth	Form
1211	Lee	Jaccck	12/11/99	11T
1225	Hughes	Amy	34/08/09	11G

a Explain the terms:

i Field

ii Record

iii File *(3 marks)*

b The data contained in the above structure contains two mistakes. One of these mistakes could have been discovered by a verification process and the other mistake by a validation process.

Fill in the table shown below by explaining what the mistake is and whether verification or validation could have detected the mistake and describe a method which could be used to prevent the error. *(6 marks)*

Description of mistake	Discovered by verification or validation?	Description of method which could have been used to prevent the mistake

Student answer 1

2 a i The information about a thing or person

ii A row in the table

iii The whole lot of information about a thing or person

b

Description of mistake	Discovered by verification or validation?	Description of method which could have been used to prevent the mistake
Wrong date of birth 34/08/09 is impossible as the days in August only go up to 31.	Validation	Range check on the days in the date to ensure it is equal to or less than 31
Forename has wrong name entered. Jaccck should be spelt Jack.	Verification	Use a spellchecker to make sure that the name is spelt correctly.

Comment

2 a i The student has defined a record here instead of a field. No marks.

ii This answer is a bit brief but worth one mark. A more complete answer would be to say that it is the details about a person, thing or transaction. An example would be the detail about one student which is a row in the table.

iii This statement is a bit vague so no mark is given. If they had given an example such as a collection of all the records about students in the school, then this would have been clearer.

b The first row of answers is all correct. The last answer about a range check is ok but if you allocate a data type of Date to a field then you cannot enter an impossible date.

The second row contains a typing error and it is not always appropriate to use spellcheckers with the names of people. The first two answers are correct for a mark each but the last answer gains no marks.

(6 marks out of 9)

Student answer 2

2 a i A field is an item of data or fact about a student. Date of birth is an example of a field.

ii A record is a collection of fields about a person or thing. In this case it is the information about a particular student.

iii A file is a complete collection of records and would be the complete records of every student in the school.

b

Description of mistake	Discovered by verification or validation?	Description of method which could have been used to prevent the mistake
Incorrect date of birth 34/08/09 This is an impossible date	Validation	Use format check for the date field. Once this is set, the user has to enter the date in a certain format e.g. DD/MM/YY.
Typing error. Jaccck should be spelt Jack.	Verification	Use a visual check to compare the data. Check by reading the entered data on the screen and correct any mistakes.

Comment

2 a i This is a good answer and notice the way the student has referred to the data in the table as an example. One mark for this.

ii Another good answer gains another mark.

iii Again another mark.

b The answers to all the parts to this answer are clear and the student has used and understood the terminology. Full marks are given for this part.

(9 marks out of 9)

Answers

2 a i One mark for a definition such as:

A field is an item of data such as surname, date of birth, etc.

ii One mark for a definition such as:

A record is a collection of fields about a person or thing

A line in the table about one particular student is a record

iii One mark for a definition such as:

A file is collection of records which forms the complete set of information about a thing or person

The details of all the records of all the students in a school is a file

b One mark for each correct answer in the table to a maximum of six marks.

Description of mistake	Discovered by verification or validation?	Description of method which could have been used to prevent the mistake
Invalid date/wrong number of days for the month/cannot have more than 31 days in a month	Validation	Use Date format/set data type to Date Use a range check/restrict day to 31 or less
Typing error/transcription error Jaccck should be Jack.	Verification	Use a visual check/Proof-read/Get person who is the data subject to check their record. Double entry of the data.

Topic 9

Communication

WORKED EXAMPLE

A software developer is working as part of a team of ten developers who are developing new software for an online loans company. The team members work in different parts of the country. The developers need to keep in touch with each other and need to pass work (mainly programs, screen designs, etc.) to each other.

a Explain **three** advantages of the developers contacting each other by email rather than by post. *(6 marks)*

b Describe **two** facilities provided by email software that will make it a lot easier to work as a team. *(4 marks)*

Student answer 1

a Cheaper

Faster

Better

b Being able to send the email to more than one person

Being able to attach a file to an email

Comment

a The word 'explain' means that a one word answer is not enough. There are 6 marks allocated here. One mark will be allocated to the clear explanation of the advantage with the other mark for the brief explanation of how it relates to working in teams. Avoid general words like 'better'. You need to be specific. General words such as faster, cheaper, better gain no marks.

(0 marks out of 6)

b 'Being able to send the email to more than one person' is a facility of email software but there needs to be a fuller explanation as to how this facility will make things easier when working as a team. It is important to tailor answers to the information given in the question.

Again 'Being able to attach a file to an email' is a facility provided by email software. There needs to be further elaboration on why this is an advantage.

(2 marks out of 4)

Student answer 2

a Sending emails speeds things up. An email can be sent and replied to in seconds, whereas a letter sent and replied to takes several days.

It is cheaper, as there is no cost for paper, printing, envelopes and stamps.

It is faster to send an email and get a reply.

ICT FOR IGCSE® TEACHER RESOURCE KIT © Oxford University Press 2012

b It is possible to create groups and send the same email to all the members of the group rather than send each email separately.

They can attach other files to the email such as programs and screen designs and this avoids them having to save them onto removable media such as CD.

Comment

a The first two answers are good answers and would get full marks.

The third answer is almost a repeat of the first answer. It is always important to check your answer is not similar to an answer already given.

(4 marks out of 6)

b Both answers are good and gain full marks.

(4 marks out of 4)

Answers

a Any three advantages (two marks each) such as:

▸▸ Email is cheaper than a letter. No stamp, envelope or paper is needed. There is also a time saving so this makes email cheaper. Even if the email is sent across the world, it will not cost any more than a local email.

▸▸ Quick to write. They are informal, meaning that people do not spend time on the layout, and the odd spelling mistake is acceptable.

▸▸ Ideal if there is a time difference. The reader can check email when they are ready.

▸▸ Inexpensive and easy to send the same email message to lots of different people.

▸▸ You can attach a copy of the sender's email with your reply, so this saves them having to search for the original message.

▸▸ You do not have to go out to a post box, so it saves time.

▸▸ You do not have to waste time shopping for stamps, envelopes and paper.

▸▸ Fast. It takes seconds to send and receive email. If the person at the other end checks their email regularly, then a reply can be sent very quickly.

b Two facilities (two marks each) such as:

▸▸ Groups/distribution lists – allowing you to send the same email to a group of people without having to select individual email addresses.

▸▸ File attachments – being able to attach files to an email so others can download the work onto their own computers and can comment on it.

Topic 11

Data manipulation

WORKED EXAMPLE

1 Yasmin has started work after leaving university and has to live away from home. She has recorded her wages and costs into a spreadsheet and this is shown here.

	A	B	C	D	E	F	G	H	I	J
1	Month	Wages	Electricity	Gas	Phone	Rent	Clothes	Food	Total costs	Money left over
2	Jan	£1,500	£60	£55	£62	£210	£40	£600	£1,027	£473
3	Feb	£1,520	£60	£55	£65	£210	£40	£600	£1,030	£490
4	Mar	£1,550	£60	£55	£64	£210	£40	£600	£1,029	£521
5	Apr	£1,550	£60	£55	£50	£210	£40	£600	£1,015	£535
6	May	£1,680	£60	£55	£47	£210	£40	£600	£1,012	£668
7	Jun	£1,690	£60	£55	£47	£210	£40	£600	£1,012	£678
8	Jul	£1,730	£60	£55	£53	£210	£40	£600	£1,018	£712
9	Aug	£1,742	£60	£55	£54	£210	£40	£600	£1,019	£723
10	Sep	£1,800	£60	£55	£62	£210	£40	£600	£1,027	£773
11	Oct	£1,800	£60	£55	£44	£210	£40	£600	£1,009	£791
12	Nov	£1,800	£60	£55	£39	£210	£40	£600	£1,004	£796
13	Dec	£1,745	£60	£55	£53	£210	£40	£600	£1,018	£727
14										

a Which one of the following formulae could be used to work out the **Total costs** in cell **I2**?

A =SUM(I2:I13)

B =I2+I3+I4+I6+I7+I8

C = SUM(B2:H2)

D =B2+C2+D2+E2+F2+H2+I2   *(1 mark)*

b Give a suitable formula that could be entered into cell J2 to work out the money Yasmin has over at the end of the month.   *(1 mark)*

c The cells apart from cells in column A and row 1 have been formatted.

   Which of the following types of cell formatting have been used for these cells?

A Euros

B Calculation

C Currency

D Right align   *(1 mark)*

d Labels are important in spreadsheets. Give the cell reference of a cell containing a label.   *(1 mark)*

e Give two advantages of Yasmin using a spreadsheet such as this to help her budget her money.   *(2 marks)*

ICT FOR IGCSE® TEACHER RESOURCE KIT   © Oxford University Press 2012

Student answer 1

1 a D

   b B2-12

   c C

   d A1

   e It is quicker

     It is more efficient

Comment

1 a When adding up cells you do not include the cell where the answer is to be put so this answer is wrong.

   b The student has forgotten to put the equals sign in front of this formula (i.e. =B2-12). This small point has cost this student a mark here.

   c This is correct so one mark here.

   d A label is any cell which describes data on the spreadsheet so this is correct and gains one mark.

   e This is a typical answer given by a weak student. The student needs to say in what way is it quicker and in what way is it more efficient. No marks for either of these answers.

     (2 marks out of 6)

Student answer 2

1 a C = SUM(B2:H2)

   b =B2-12

   c C Currency

   d Row 1

   e Provided the calculations have been set up correctly and tested, the formulae will always produce a correct calculation

     When one of the numbers in the spreadsheet is changed, the cells which depend on the changed cell will recalculate automatically

Comment

1 a This is correct so one mark here.

   b This is correct so one mark here.

   c This is correct so one mark here.

   d All the cells in row 1 do contain labels but the question asks for a cell reference so this is an incorrect answer so no marks.

   e These are both very good answers and worth a mark each.

     (5 marks out of 6)

Answers

1 **a** One mark for the letter, formula or both (i.e. C = SUM(B2:H2))

b One mark for a correct formula which must include the equals sign (i.e. =B2-I2).

c One mark for C Currency.

d One mark for any cell reference in row 1 or column A. It must be a cell reference and not a column letter or row number.

e One mark for each of two advantages of a spreadsheet such as:

If set up correctly, the formulae will always produce a correct calculation.

Automatic recalculation when numbers are changed in the spreadsheet.

Once the spreadsheet has been set up, the spreadsheet can be reused for different years by putting in different data.

The data can easily be represented pictorially by getting the spreadsheet to produce graphs and charts.

You can change the information in the spreadsheet in order to make and test 'what if' scenarios.

Topic 16

Presentation authoring

WORKED EXAMPLE

1 A presentation is to be used by visitors to a castle. The idea is that users will be able to find out about the history of the castle and what it was like to live in a castle in that era.

Explain how each of the following could be used in the design of this presentation.

a   Animations   *(2 marks)*

b   Links   *(2 marks)*

c   Slide transitions   *(2 marks)*

Student answer 1

1   a   Use moving things
        Makes it better

    b   You can move from one slide to another
        The user can click on a hot spot

    c   The material on the slide can shoot in from the side of the slide
        It makes it exciting for the user

Comment

1   a   This is a vague and poor answer and no marks are awarded.

    b   Both of these are valid answers and one mark is awarded for it.

    c   Material such as bullet points shooting onto the slide is not really an example of slide transition as the slide is already on the screen. One mark (just) is given for the second answer.

        (2 marks out of 6)

Student answer 2

1   a   Use moving images showing what is in each room.
        Have a heading showing the names of the castle which moves from left to right.

    b   Allow the user to decide what they want to see next by allowing them to click on links which take them to other pages.
        Links could be used to allow the user to virtually visit each of the rooms and look around.

    c   These are pictures around the edge of a slide.
        You can sometimes find these included with clip art.

Comment

1 a These are both suitable examples so two marks are awarded.

   b These two very good answers explaining how links might be used is awarded two marks.

   c What the student has described here are borders. Slide transitions are the way one slide is removed and the next slide appears. No marks for this answer.

   (4 marks out of 6)

Answers

1 a One mark for each point (NB must be a sensible use of animation) to a maximum of two marks.

   Have a cartoon showing what life was like

   Use animation to show how certain parts of the castle were used

   Etc.

   b One mark for each point to a maximum of two marks.

   Link to an aerial view such as Google Earth

   Link to other pages in the presentation

   Link to the Internet so that they can access further information

   Etc.

   c One mark for each point to a maximum of two marks.

   Have one slide fading as another slide appears

   Have one slide shooting in from the side

   Etc.

ICT FOR IGCSE® TEACHER RESOURCE KIT   © Oxford University Press 2012

Revision material

The following material will help with revision for the Paper 1 examination.

Can you work out what the word is?

Here are some words or phrases which have been jumbled up. The words are connected with software. Can you work out what they are? There is a clue to help you.

1 Desert phase

Hint: Software good for manipulating numerical data.

Answer: _____

2 Progress cod win

Hint: Software you would write a letter with.

Answer: _____

3 Shipbuild kept song

Hint: Software good for combing text and graphics.

Answer: _____

4 Patient snore

Hint: Software used to present material on slides.

Answer: _____

5 Plastic piano

Hint: Type of software used to do a specific job.

Answer: _____

6 Generosity stamp

Hint: Software that controls the hardware directly.

Answer: _____

Worksheet R1 (continued)

7   Romp rag

Hint: Step by step instructions.

Answer: _____

8   Abase tad

Hint: Software that puts data into a certain structure.

Answer: _____

9   Woodland

Hint: Obtaining software using the Internet.

Answer: _____

10   Ray poll

Hint: Program used for working out wages.

Answer: _____

Worksheet R2

The Internet

What do these terms mean?

Here is a list of terms in alphabetical order. Put the meanings next to the term.
If you don't know what the meaning is, then use one of the glossaries available on the Internet.

Term	Meaning
Browser	
Cookie	
Download	
Email	
FAQ	
HTML	
Hacker	
ISP	
Link	
Surfing	
User-ID	
Web page	

Revision questions Paper 1

The following questions will help you revise the content for Paper 1.

1 Here are some different methods of entering data into a computer:

OMR	**MICR**	**magnetic stripe**	**bar codes**
keyboard	**sensors**	**voice recognition**	**mouse**

Using the list above, choose the best method of data capture for each of the following situations:

a For inputting credit card details when customers are paying for goods in a supermarket.

_____

b To use with a graphical user interface.

_____

c For obtaining temperature measurements in a greenhouse.

_____

d For recording the answers on a multiple choice answer sheet.

_____

e For dictating a story direct into a word-processor.

_____

f To record the details of items being sold in a supermarket.

_____   [6]

2 a Describe what is meant by the term batch processing?

_____

_____

_____

_____

[2]

b Give the names of two applications that are ideally suited to batch processing.

_____

_____

[2]

c Describe what is meant by the term real-time processing?

_____

_____

_____

[2]

d Give the names of two applications that are ideally suited to real-time processing.

_____

_____

[2]

3 Place a tick in the boxes that contain tasks performed by the operating system of a computer.

Task	Put a tick here if the task is performed by the operating system.
Performing calculations in a spreadsheet	
Managing space for files on the disk drive	
Issuing an instruction to the printer to start printing	
Formatting text in a word-processed document	
Accepting the input from a mouse	
Spellchecking a document	
Copying a file from one disk to another	

[4]

4 Hospitals make use of ICT systems for keeping patient records. Apart from contact details such as name, address, postcode and telephone numbers, give **four** distinctly different fields that would be included in a patient database and describe why they are needed.

_____

_____

_____

_____

_____

_____

_____

_____

_____

_____

_____

_____

_____

_____

_____

_____

_____

_____

_____

_____

_____

_____

[8]

5 Loyalty schemes are very popular in stores for encouraging shoppers to make purchases at the store on a regular basis. When customers join the scheme they fill in an application form and when this is done, the details are entered into a database and a plastic card containing a magnetic stripe is sent by post to the customer.

When customer details are entered into a database they are verified and validated.

a Define the term verification. Name and describe **one** verification method that can be used during the entry of customer data.

_____

_____

_____

_____

[3]

b Define the term validation. Name and describe **one** validation method used during the entry of customer data.

_____

_____

_____

_____

[3]

6 Here are some descriptions of methods of verification and validation. You have to state whether each one represents verification or validation.

a Two operators typing the same data in twice. Only if the data is exactly the same, will it be accepted for processing.

_____ [1]

b Making sure that an employee number is entered into a field before the payroll details can be processed.

_____ [1]

c Checking an order after it has been typed in by reading the paper order and seeing if it is exactly the same as what is on the screen.

_____ [1]

d A program that makes sure that the amount for a gas bill is not ridiculously large.

_____ [1]

7 Tick (√) the correct column to show whether each of the following statements about health risks in using ICT is true or false.

	True	False
The continual use of keyboards over a long period can give rise to aches and pains in the hands, arms and wrists		
RSI stands for repeated stress injury		
Wrist rests and ergonomic keyboards can help prevent RSI		
Back ache can be caused by slouching in your chair when using a computer		
Glare on the screen can cause RSI		

[5]

8 It is important to fully document a system. For each of the following types of system documentation, put a tick in the relevant box to indicate whether it is technical or user documentation.

	Technical	User
Test plans		
Trouble-shooting guide		
Program coding/Program listing		
File structures		
Frequently asked questions (FAQ)		

ICT FOR IGCSE® TEACHER RESOURCE KIT   © Oxford University Press 2012

System flowcharts		
How to log in and log out of the system		
The hardware requirements to run the system		
Tutorials to explain how to use the system		

[9]

9 A heated greenhouse in a normally cold country is being used to grow tropical fruit. They want the growing conditions inside the greenhouse to be controlled automatically using a computer.

   a Give the names of **three** sensors that they would need to use to measure the soil and growing conditions.

   _____

   _____

[3]

   b Output devices will be needed to control the growing conditions. Describe **three** output devices that they would need to control the growing conditions.

   _____

   _____

   _____

   _____

   _____

[3]

   c Describe the computer processing which would be required to maintain the necessary growing conditions.

   _____

   _____

   _____

   _____

   _____

   _____

   _____

   _____

[5]

   d Computers are used to control the conditions inside the greenhouse. Explain why computers are used rather than humans for this purpose.

   _____

   _____

   _____

   _____

[3]

10 A small network is to be created in a home so that all the computers can share files and an Internet connection. Explain why each of the following devices would be needed.

   A router _____

   _____

   A browser _____

   _____

Email _____

_____

An ISP _____

_____

[4]

11 More people are using the Internet for booking holidays and theatre tickets as well as for banking. Discuss this development and explain the effect it is having on ordinary people and their lives.

_____

_____

_____

_____

_____

_____

_____

_____

_____

_____

_____

_____

[8]

12 The Internet has allowed many new services to be developed. Two such services are blogs and wikis.

   a Give **two** features of a wiki.

_____

_____

[2]

   b Give **two** features of a blog.

_____

_____

[2]

13 Describe the differences between a LAN and a WAN. [5]

_____

_____

_____

_____

_____

_____

_____

_____

[5]

Answers

Worksheet R1

Can you work out what the word is?

1 Spreadsheet
2 Word processing
3 Desk top publishing
4 Presentation
5 Application
6 Operating system
7 Program
8 Database
9 Download
10 Payroll

Worksheet R2

The Internet

Term	Meaning
Browser	Software used to search for information using the Internet.
Cookie	A small program which monitors your searching activity.
Download	Obtaining a file off the Internet and saving it on your own computer.
Email	A electronic message sent over a network which is usually the Internet.
FAQ	Frequently Ask Questions. A list of the questions the people who use a web site most often ask, along with the answers.
HTML	A list of instructions on how to display the content of a web page.
Hacker	A person who gains illegal access to a computer system.
ISP	Internet service provider. The people who provide you with your Internet connection.
Link	A way of moving from one place to another on the Internet.
Surfing	Moving around different web pages and web sites using the links on the Internet.
User-ID	A name given to you or that you give yourself so that you are recognized by the system.
Web page	A document/page which has been uploaded to enable it to be accessed by anyone using the Internet.

Revision questions Paper 1

1 One mark for each correct answer:
a Magnetic stripe
b Mouse
c Sensors
d OMR
e Voice recognition
f Bar codes

2 a Any two marks allocated in the following way:

Is where all the inputs are collected over a period of time (1) and then batched and processed in one go (1). The inputs are processed automatically to produce the output (1).

b One mark each for two of the following:

Producing attendance statistics from attendances recorded on OMR forms

Producing bills for water, gas, telephone and electricity companies

Producing monthly bank or credit card statements

Marking multiple-choice examination papers

c Any two marks allocated in the following way:

Processing which is done immediately without any delay (1). The system responds immediately and alters the system in some way (1). Because the data from these systems must be received and processed immediately, sensors are used to collect the data (1).

d One mark each for two of the following:

Flood warning systems

Autopilots for aircraft

Computer games

Traffic light control

Process control in factories (i.e., making steel, chemical plants, etc.)

Controlling robots

3 One mark for each correctly placed tick.

Task	Put a tick here if the task is performed by the operating system.
Performing calculations in a spreadsheet	
Managing space for files on the hard disk	√
Issuing an instruction to the printer to start printing	√
Formatting text in a word-processed document	
Accepting the input from a mouse	√
Spellchecking a document	
Copying a file from one folder to another	√

4 One mark for the name of the field and one mark for the correct description. Candidates must supply a sensible field in the context of a patient record and a correct explanation. Any contact details for the patient gain no marks.

DOB – so that their age can be calculated – important when calculating dosages of drugs

Next of kin – in case they need to be contacted re deteriorating condition, death, etc.

Allergies – so doctors can ensure certain drugs are not given that the patient is allergic to

Medication – doctors can see the drugs the patient is taking to make sure suitable drugs are prescribed

Current GP – so the family doctor can be contacted with information about the patient's treatment

Patient number – used to identify a particular patient to the computer system

Operations – details of any operations the patient has had in their lifetime so the doctors are able to make a correct diagnosis

Medical conditions – doctors treating one medical condition will need to know other conditions the patient suffers from

5 **a** One mark for a suitable definition such as:

Verification means checking that the data being entered into the ICT system perfectly matches the source of the data.

No mark for the name of the method but up to two marks for the description.

Proof-reading/visual check – carefully reading what they have typed in (1) and comparing it with what is on the data source/application form to find errors (1).

Double entry of data – two people use the same data source to enter the details into the database (1) and only if the two sets of data are identical, will they be accepted for processing (1).

b One mark for a suitable definition such as:

Validation – the process which ensures that data accepted for processing is sensible and reasonable.

No mark for the name of the method but up to two marks for the description.

Presence checks – some database fields have to be filled in whilst others can be left empty (1) so if data for an essential field is left blank, the data for the other fields will not be accepted for processing (1).

Data type checks – check if the data being entered is the same type as the data type specified for the field (1). This would check to make sure that only numbers are entered into fields specified as numeric (1).

Range checks – are performed on numbers to check that a number being entered is within a certain range (1). For example, if you have to be over a certain age to have a loyalty card then if a date of birth were entered and this gave an age less than this, the data entry would not be allowed by the range check (1).

Format checks – are performed on codes to make sure that they conform to the correct combinations of characters (1). For example, a date of birth may have to be in a certain format (e.g. dd/mm/yy) and unless it is in the correct format it will be rejected (1).

6 One mark for each correct answer.

a Verification

b Validation

c Verification

d Validation

7 One mark for each tick placed in the correct column.

	True	False
The continual use of keyboards over a long period can give rise to aches and pains in the hands, arms and wrists.	√	
RSI stands for Repeated Stress Injury		√
Wrist rests and ergonomic keyboards can help prevent RSI	√	
Back ache can be caused by slouching in your chair when using a computer	√	
Glare on the screen can cause RSI		√

8 One mark for each tick placed in the correct column.

	Technical	User
Test plans	√	
Trouble-shooting guide		√
Program coding/Program listing	√	
File structures	√	
Frequently asked questions (FAQ)		√
System flowcharts	√	
How to log in and log out of the system		√
The hardware requirements to run the system		√
Tutorials to explain how to use the system		√

9 a One mark for each of three sensors from:

Moisture

Humidity

Temperature

Light

pH

Gas (oxygen or carbon dioxide)

b One mark for each description:

Buzzer – to warn if the conditions go outside the ideal conditions (e.g. if the temperature is too low).

Heaters – will turn on if the temperature is too cold and turn off if it is too hot.

Air conditioner – will cool the greenhouse down if it gets too hot.

Light bulb – will supply artificial light if the outside light intensity falls.

Motors – will open the windows if the humidity is too high or the temperature is too high and close if they are too low.

Fan – used to reduce the temperature if it gets too hot.

c Max of five points from:

A temperature sensor continually monitors the temperature and sends a reading to the processor at regular intervals.

It is compared with a stored value to see whether it is too high or low.

If the temperature is lower than the stored value then a signal is sent to the heater to switch it on.

If the temperature is lower than the stored value then a signal is sent to the motor to shut the windows if they are open.

If the temperature is higher than the stored value then a signal is sent to the heater to switch it off.

If the temperature is higher than the stored value and the windows are shut then a signal is sent to the motor to open them.

If the temperature is higher than the stored value then a signal is sent to turn on the fan.

A light sensor continually monitors the light level and sends a reading to the processor at regular intervals.

The light level is compared with the stored value.

If the light level is less than the stored value the processor sends an instruction to turn the light on.

If the light level is greater than the stored value and the light is on, then an instruction is given to turn it off.

A moisture sensor continually monitors moisture readings and sends a reading to the processor at regular intervals.

The moisture level is compared with the stored value.

If the moisture level is too low an instruction is sent by the processor to switch on the sprinkler.

If the moisture level is too high and the sprinkler is on then the processor turns the sprinkler off.

d Three explanations from:

The computer can control the conditions 24 hours per day.

It is cheaper as humans do not have to be paid to control the conditions.

The response time of the computer is faster so it is able to control the conditions more accurately.

Computers can take readings more frequently.

10 One mark for each correct answer:

A router – enables all the computers in the network to share a single link to the Internet

A browser – software that can be used to find and display web pages and to access resources on the Internet

Email – method of sending digital messages from one person to another

An ISP – an organization which supplies users with a permanent connection to the Internet

11 Eight from:

Advantages

Do not have to waste time travelling to banks/shops/travel agents/theatres

Disabled people can gain their independence because they do not have to rely on others

Less pollution as fewer car journeys are needed

Much greater choice of products/holidays to choose from

Can book/shop/bank 24/7

Do not have to queue up to pay for goods/services

No travelling expenses (e.g. fares, petrol, car parking)

Disadvantages

No social interaction

Not everyone has a computer or connection to the Internet

Hackers may gain access to your credit card/banking details

Some sites are bogus and are used to steal your money

If you buy clothes you have the hassle of sending them back if they do not fit or suit you

You cannot get the goods immediately because you usually have to wait for delivery

There is no personal touch

Can only have a max of 5 marks from either advantages or disadvantages.

12 a One mark each for two points:

A wiki is a web page

It can be viewed and modified by anyone who has a web browser

b One mark for each of two points:

An online journal or diary of events in the form of a website

They are interactive and allow a visitor to leave comments

13 One mark for each difference to a maximum of five marks:

LAN is confined to a small area/WAN covers a wide geographical area such as between cities, countries, etc.

LAN is located in a single building or site/WAN covers lots of buildings such as branches.

LAN uses cable, wireless, infra-red and microwave links which are usually owned by the organization whereas WANs use expensive telecommunications equipment such as satellite links.

LANs are cheaper to build as the organization owns the networking equipment. WANs are more expensive because of the cost of services from telecoms companies.

LANs have lower speed connections because the amount of data transferred across the network is small. WANs have high amounts of data transfer so need fast connections.

LANs are cheaper to run as they are simple, whereas WANs need specialist staff who are highly paid.

Revision tips

Here are some revision tips which will hopefully help you to maximize your mark in the examinations for both theory and practical.

In the student book, Topics 1 to 8 cover the theory needed for Paper 1 of the examination. There will be some questions on communication, spreadsheets, databases and other material on Paper 1, but you will gain the knowledge needed by attempting all the practical work.

The practical work for Paper 2 and Paper 3 of the examination is covered in Topics 9 to 16 of the student book.

How do I revise?

Everyone has their own way of revising but here are a few tips which might help:

- Start your revision early. Remember you will have lots of other subjects to revise nearer exam time.
- Work at a table or desk with bright light.
- Work somewhere quiet where there will not be any distractions.
- Write brief notes out. You tend to remember more of what you write compared to what you read.
- Make a plan of how much revision you will do and the times you will do it. Try to stick to this.
- Try to get up early. If you complete your revision, you have the rest of the day to enjoy yourself.
- Get friends/relatives to test you. You could give them the glossary at the back of the book to test you on definitions of terms.
- Read carefully the following tips and remember to apply them in the examination.
- Print a copy of the syllabus out. You can get a copy from the University of Cambridge International Examinations website. Use this as a good summary of what you have to learn. Many students like to highlight the material using a pen when they have thoroughly understood the material.
- Learn all the facts, terms and concepts in the syllabus.
- Do not simply memorize the material as you may have to apply the concepts to a situation asked in a question.
- There are many questions in the student book, including many IGCSE past questions. You can test yourself by answering them and then marking them yourself using the answers which are supplied in the *Teacher Resource Kit* which your teacher is likely to have.
- Use your teacher/lecturer. If you do not understand something, do not be afraid to ask them.
- Use past papers, some of which can be obtained from the University of Cambridge International Examinations website, to help you revise. You will also be able to obtain some mark schemes for the examination off the website. Your teacher will be able to supply you with recent past papers and mark schemes. The more you understand about the way these papers are marked, the more marks you will get in your examinations.
- Make sure that you understand the differences between the command words used on the examination papers. These words include name/give/describe/discuss/explain.

Before the exam

Here are some things you should do on the days of the examinations:

▸▸ Collect the necessary equipment: two pens (in case one dries up); two pencils; a sharpener; a rubber; and a ruler.

▸▸ Always take a watch into the exam. There will be a clock in the exam room but if you are at the back you might not be able to see it.

▸▸ Go to the toilet before the exam; this avoids the embarrassment of having to leave the room under supervision.

▸▸ Check to see if you have to wear school uniform.

Tips for Paper 1

▸▸ Always read the instructions on the front of the paper carefully. In particular, note the time you are allowed. Read the question carefully before answering. Ensure that your answer is the answer to the precise question being asked. Too many students see a key word and then write everything they know about it.

▸▸ Do not write any irrelevant information in answer to a question. You will not gain marks and simply penalize yourself by the time you waste.

▸▸ Allocate your time sensibly. Use the mark scheme at the side of the questions as a guide to how much you should write. If there are, say, two marks, there must be two points you need to mention in order to get both marks.

▸▸ Try to write neatly. The examiners have hundreds of scripts to mark and it is not worth risking annoying an examiner by making her/him waste time deciphering an untidy script.

▸▸ Only do what the question asks. If it asks for two reasons, make sure that you give two: not three or one. Always check that, in an answer to a question with two parts, you have not written similar answers to both parts. If you have, you will only obtain marks for one of them.

▸▸ After you have answered a question, read it through again to make sure that you have not missed part of it out.

▸▸ Make sure that you answer all the questions on the paper. If you leave a question out to answer later, you must remember to go back to it.

▸▸ Do not give your answer as a series of notes or bullet points. Your answers should be given, where appropriate, in complete sentences.

▸▸ If a question asks you to give an example in an answer then not giving an example will cost you marks.

▸▸ Read the whole question carefully before you start to answer. This is to avoid giving too much information in one of the answers which should have been given as an answer to a later part of the same question.

Understanding what the question means

There are certain command words used in questions and it is important to understand what they mean. If you write too much you will waste time. If you write too little you will lose marks. You need to write the correct amount. Here is what each command word means.

Name

A one-word answer would be acceptable but it is better to use a phrase wherever possible.

Give

Here you have to provide the person marking the question more information than a single-word statement.

Describe

This means that you should give a detailed answer. If there are four marks allocated, then make sure that you write a minimum of four sentences with each covering a different aspect of the answer. You have to convince the person marking the question that you can describe an answer that is appropriate to the question.

Define

This usually means explain a technical term in language that anyone could understand.

Explain/Give reasons

Explain means saying why certain things happen as opposed to describing what happens. You need to give an answer in sentences here and ensure the reasons why something happens are clear. If you simply say what happens, you will not gain the marks.

Discuss

Discuss usually involves writing down both the advantages and the disadvantages to show both sides of an argument in a given situation. As well as doing this, you should also come to a conclusion.

The practical papers: things you must do when submitting your work for the practical exams

▸▸ Make sure that you obey the instructions on the paper.

▸▸ Make sure that your name and other details, such as candidate number, as specified on the exam paper are included on every printout you produce. If you do not put your name on a printout it will not be marked.

▸▸ If you have a printout which you do not want to be marked, you must cross out the work.

▸▸ You will probably practise the practical work by completing previous examination papers. This is a good idea but you must not rely on the examination paper you do being similar to a previous one. You must be able to adapt your knowledge or software and the practical skills you have gained to new situations.

▸▸ Read the paper carefully from start to finish before starting to complete the questions. This will give you an overview and you can think about the skills you will need to use in your answers.

Mindmaps

Although students should be made aware that they can't use mindmaps as answers in an examination, they can be useful to consolidate learning.

Topic 1

Types and components of computer systems

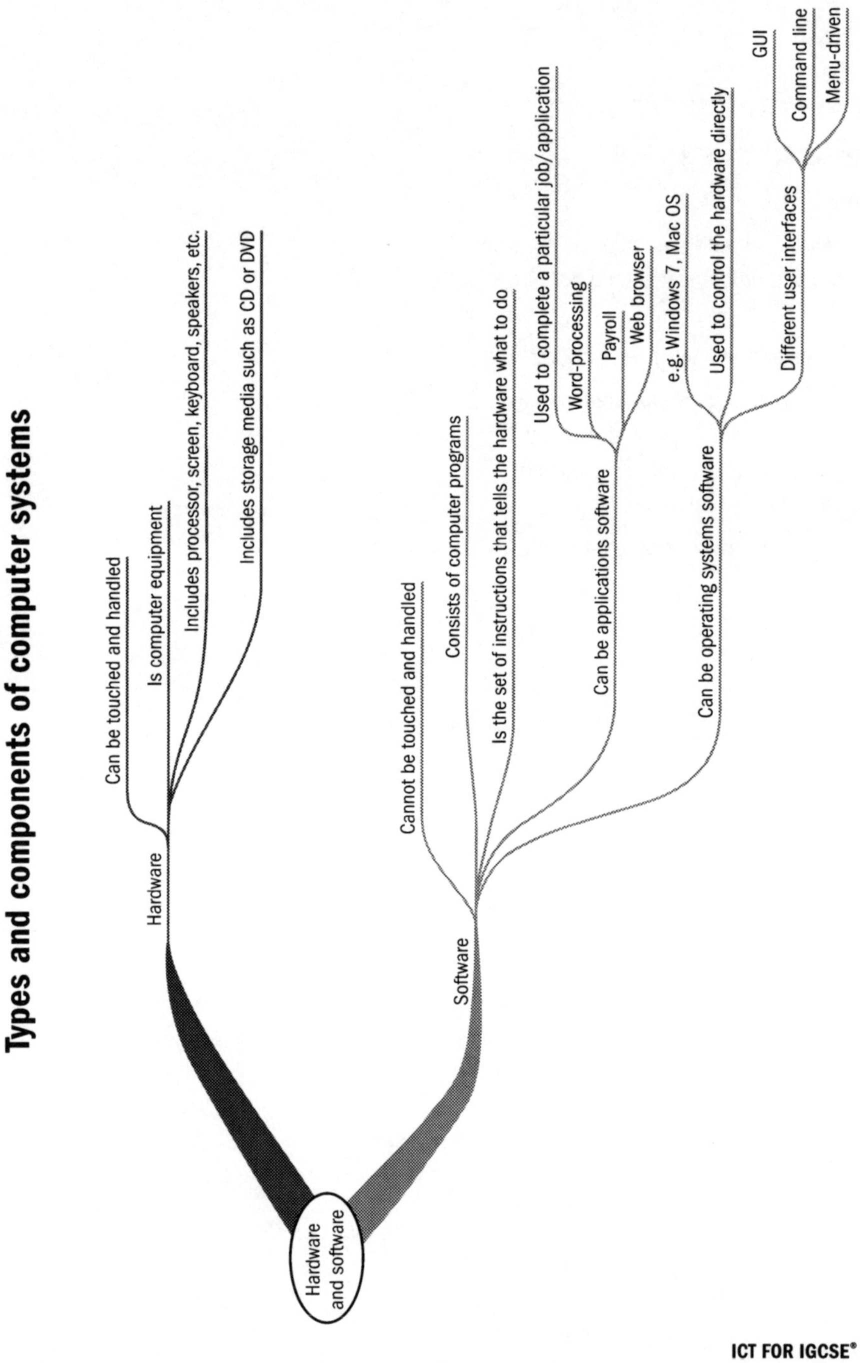

Types and components of computer systems

- Hardware
  - Can be touched and handled
  - Is computer equipment
    - Includes processor, screen, keyboard, speakers, etc.
    - Includes storage media such as CD or DVD
- Software
  - Cannot be touched and handled
  - Consists of computer programs
  - Is the set of instructions that tells the hardware what to do
  - Can be applications software
    - Used to complete a particular job/application
      - Word-processing
      - Payroll
      - Web browser
  - Can be operating systems software
    - e.g. Windows 7, Mac OS
    - Used to control the hardware directly
    - Different user interfaces
      - GUI
      - Command line
      - Menu-driven

Hardware and software

ICT FOR IGCSE® TEACHER RESOURCE KIT   © Oxford University Press 2012

Main functions of an operating system

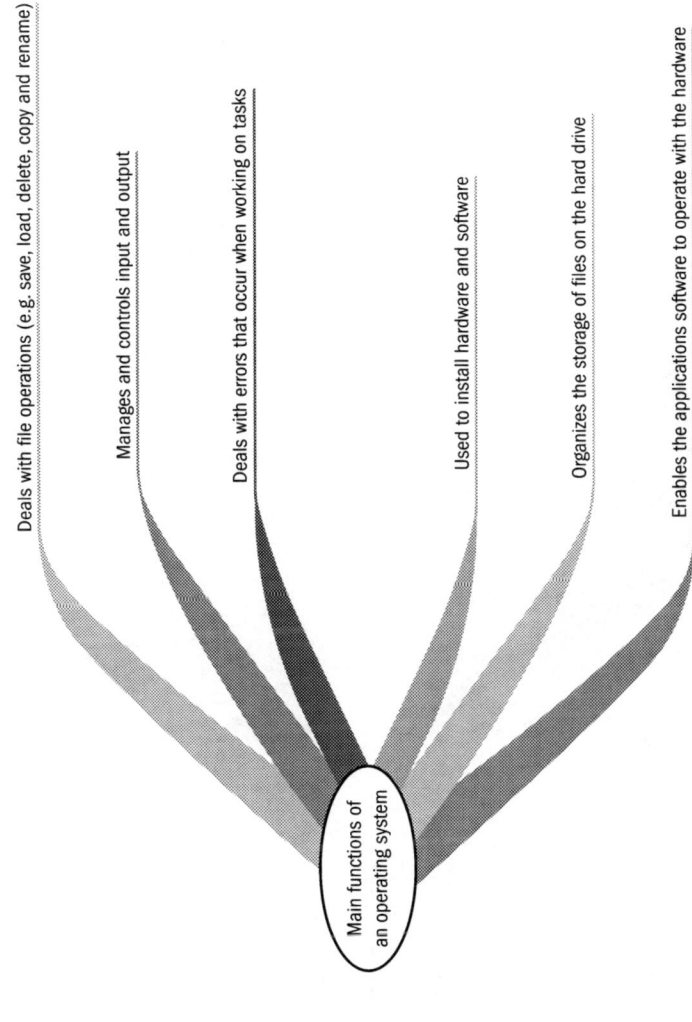

Deals with file operations (e.g. save, load, delete, copy and rename)

Manages and controls input and output

Deals with errors that occur when working on tasks

Used to install hardware and software

Organizes the storage of files on the hard drive

Enables the applications software to operate with the hardware

Main functions of an operating system

Topic 2

Input and output devices

Input devices

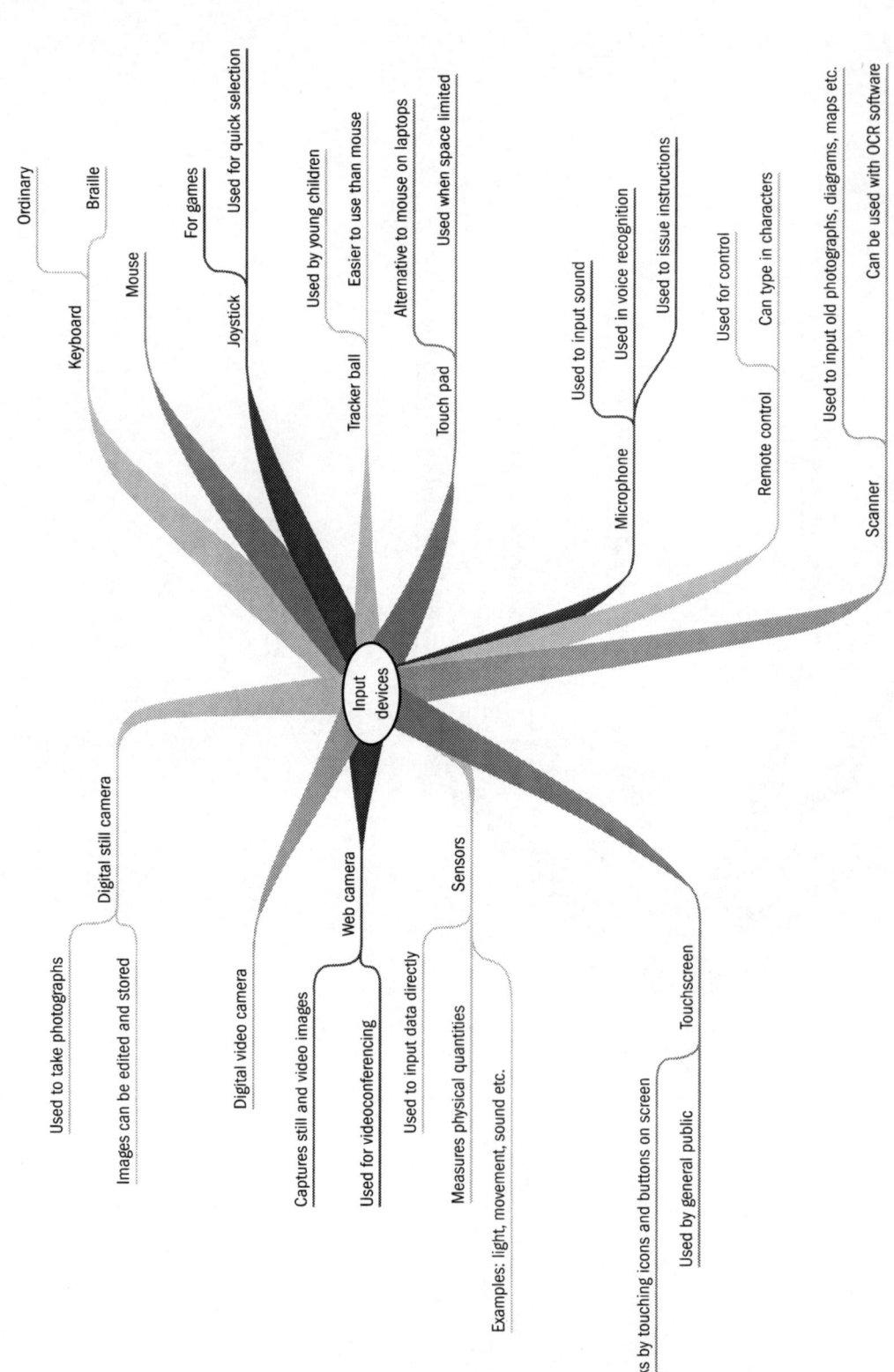

- Input devices
  - Keyboard
    - Ordinary
    - Braille
  - Mouse
    - Used for quick selection
  - Joystick
    - For games
  - Tracker ball
    - Used by young children
    - Easier to use than mouse
  - Touch pad
    - Alternative to mouse on laptops
    - Used when space limited
  - Microphone
    - Used to input sound
    - Used in voice recognition
  - Remote control
    - Used to issue instructions
    - Used for control
  - Scanner
    - Can type in characters
    - Used to input old photographs, diagrams, maps etc.
    - Can be used with OCR software
  - Digital still camera
    - Used to take photographs
    - Images can be edited and stored
  - Web camera
    - Digital video camera
    - Captures still and video images
    - Used for videoconferencing
  - Sensors
    - Used to input data directly
    - Measures physical quantities
    - Examples: light, movement, sound etc.
  - Touchscreen
    - Works by touching icons and buttons on screen
    - Used by general public

ICT FOR IGCSE® TEACHER RESOURCE KIT   © Oxford University Press 2012

More specialist input devices

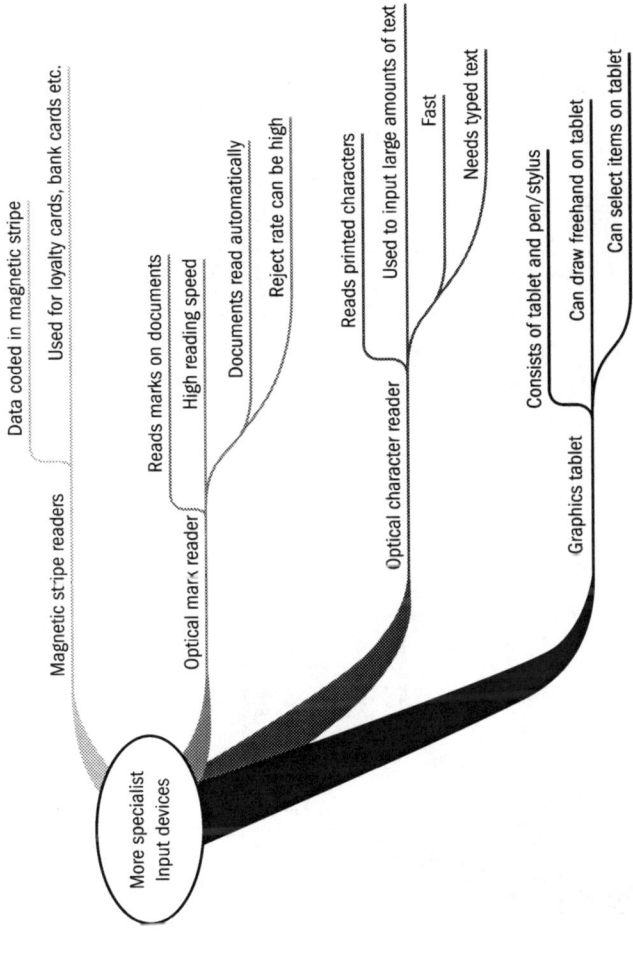

- More specialist Input devices
  - Magnetic stripe readers
    - Data coded in magnetic stripe
    - Used for loyalty cards, bank cards etc.
  - Optical mark reader
    - Reads marks on documents
    - High reading speed
    - Documents read automatically
    - Reject rate can be high
  - Optical character reader
    - Reads printed characters
    - Used to input large amounts of text
    - Fast
    - Needs typed text
  - Graphics tablet
    - Consists of tablet and pen/stylus
    - Can draw freehand on tablet
    - Can select items on tablet

Output devices

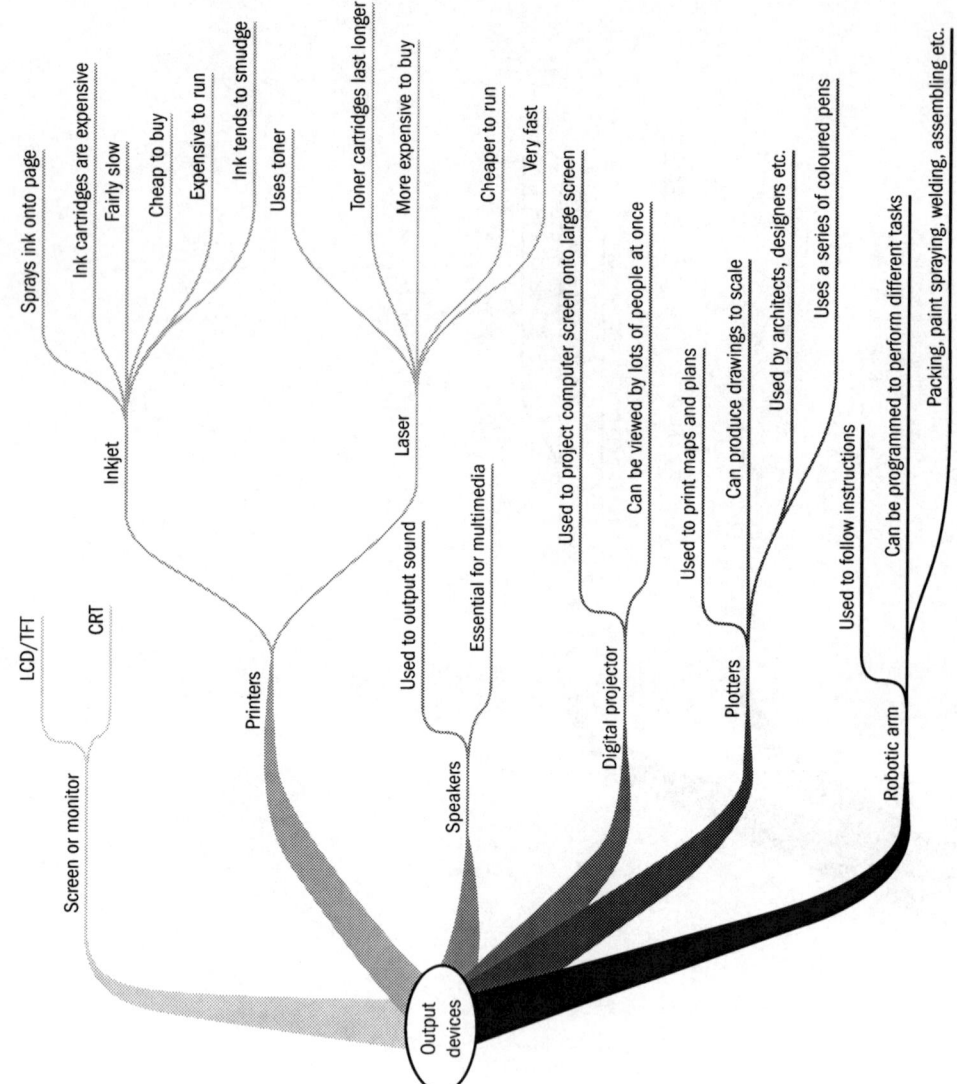

Output devices

- Screen or monitor
  - LCD/TFT
  - CRT
- Printers
  - Inkjet
    - Sprays ink onto page
    - Ink cartridges are expensive
    - Fairly slow
    - Cheap to buy
    - Expensive to run
    - Ink tends to smudge
  - Laser
    - Uses toner
    - Toner cartridges last longer
    - More expensive to buy
    - Cheaper to run
    - Very fast
- Speakers
  - Used to output sound
  - Essential for multimedia
- Digital projector
  - Used to project computer screen onto large screen
  - Can be viewed by lots of people at once
- Plotters
  - Used to print maps and plans
  - Can produce drawings to scale
  - Used by architects, designers etc.
  - Uses a series of coloured pens
- Robotic arm
  - Used to follow instructions
  - Can be programmed to perform different tasks
  - Packing, paint spraying, welding, assembling etc.

Topic 3

Storage devices and media

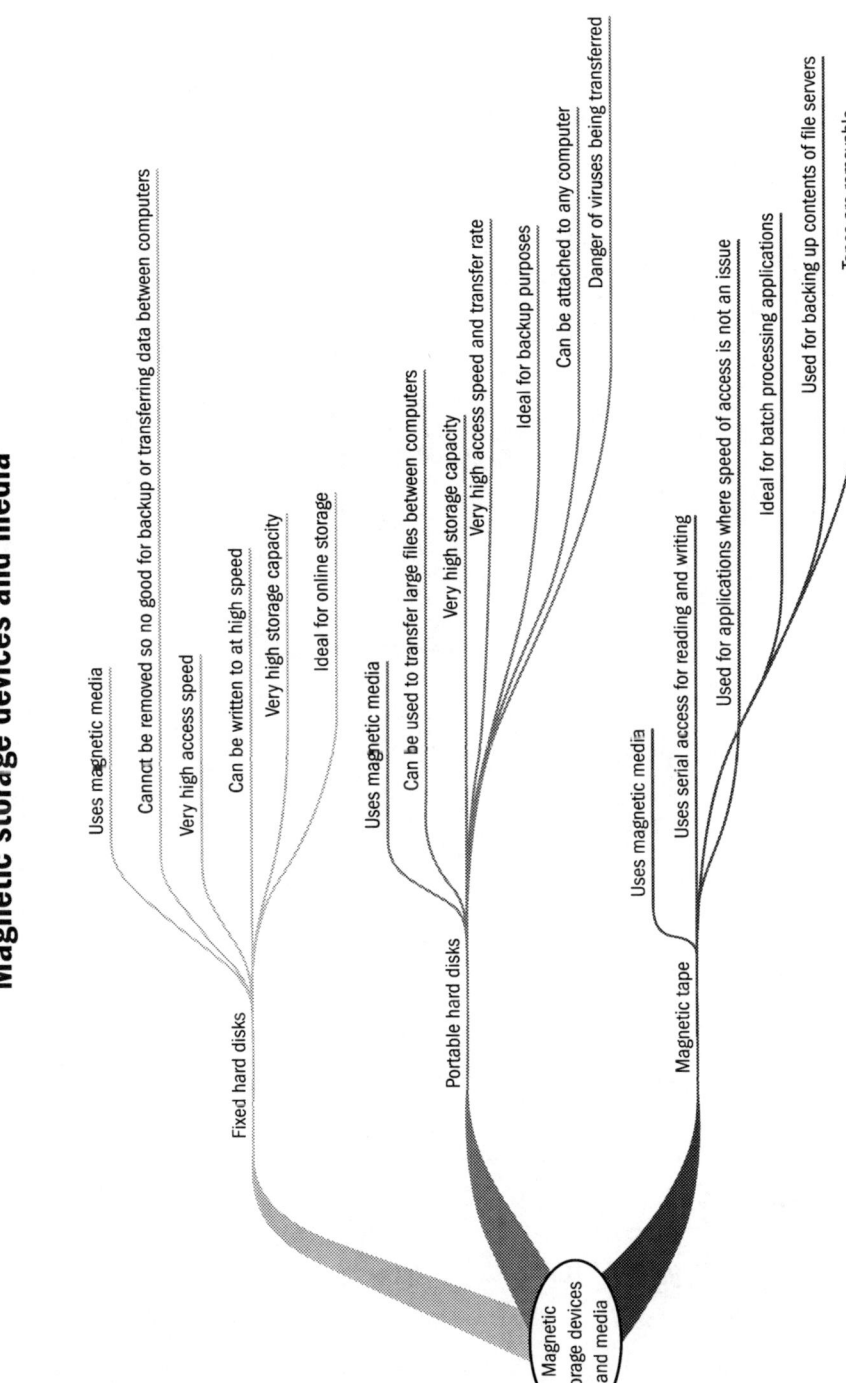

Magnetic storage devices and media

- **Fixed hard disks**
  - Uses magnetic media
  - Cannot be removed so no good for backup or transferring data between computers
  - Very high access speed
  - Can be written to at high speed
  - Very high storage capacity
  - Ideal for online storage

- **Portable hard disks**
  - Uses magnetic media
  - Can be used to transfer large files between computers
  - Very high storage capacity
  - Very high access speed and transfer rate
  - Ideal for backup purposes
  - Can be attached to any computer
  - Danger of viruses being transferred

- **Magnetic tape**
  - Uses magnetic media
  - Uses serial access for reading and writing
  - Used for applications where speed of access is not an issue
  - Ideal for batch processing applications
  - Used for backing up contents of file servers
  - Tapes are removable

Magnetic storage devices and media

Optical and solid state backing storage devices

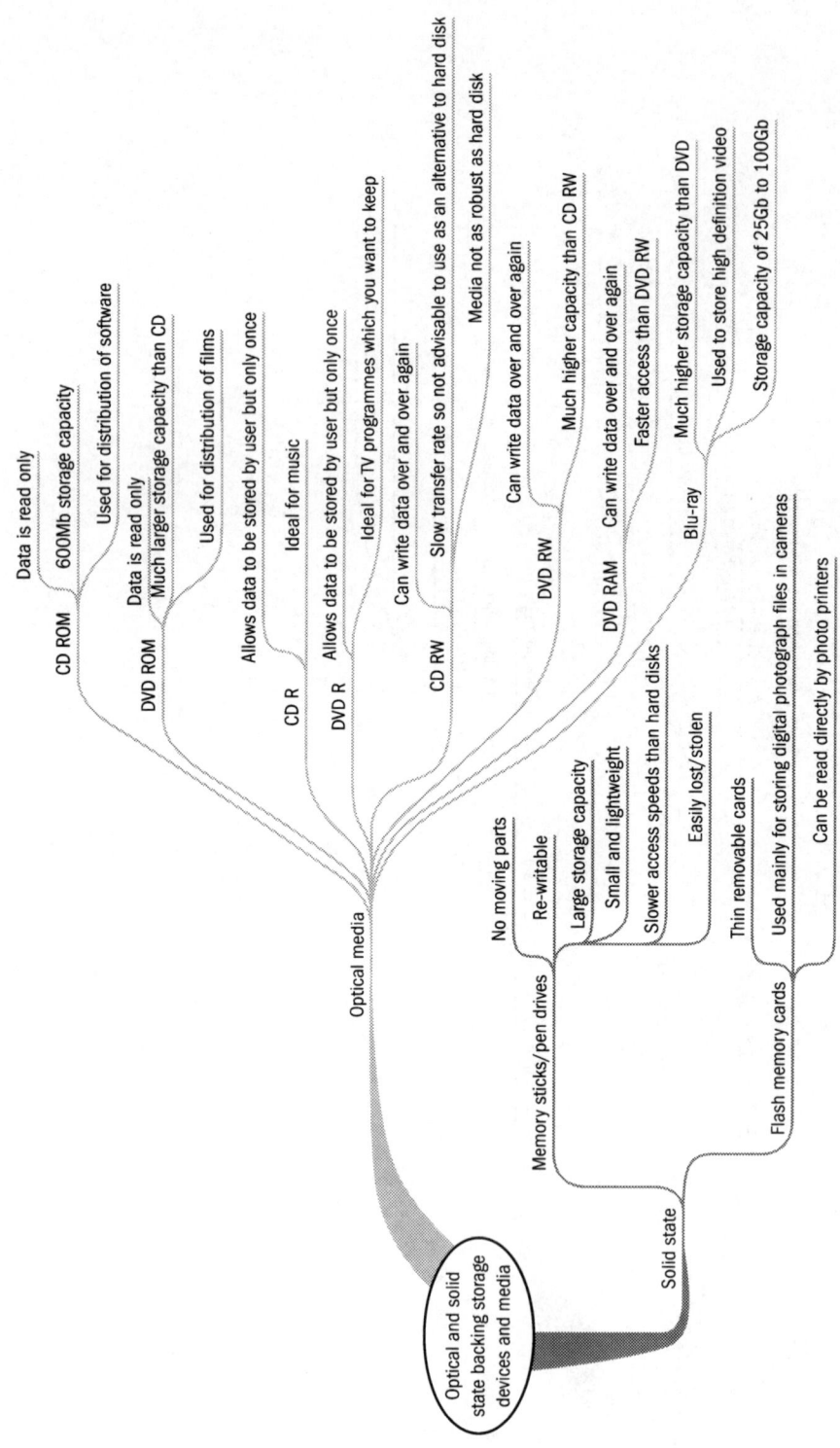

Topic 4

Computer networks

Types of network (LANs and WANs)

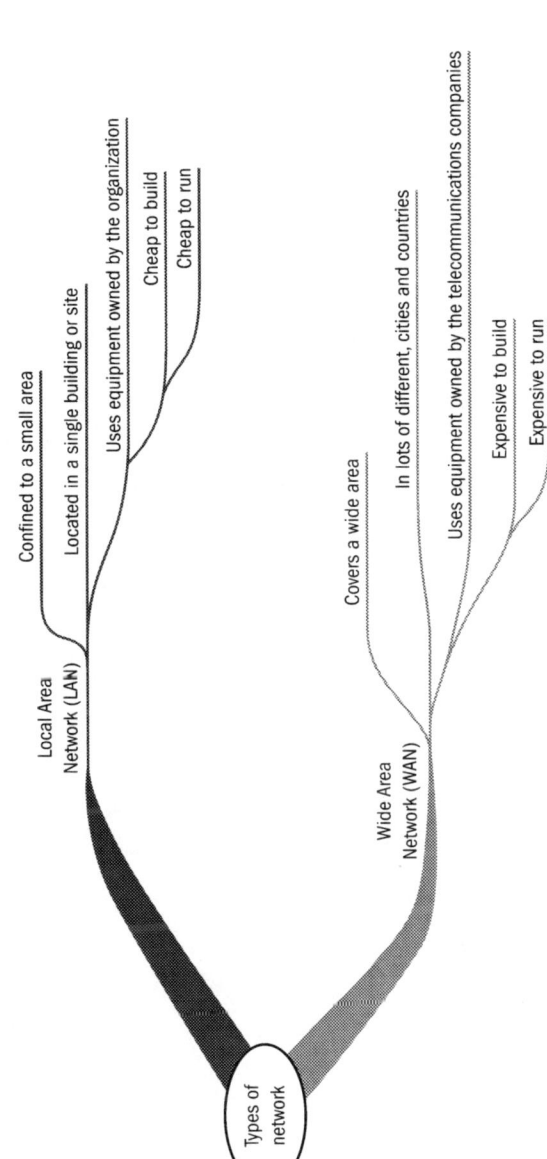

Types of network

Local Area Network (LAN)
- Confined to a small area
- Located in a single building or site
- Uses equipment owned by the organization
  - Cheap to build
  - Cheap to run

Wide Area Network (WAN)
- Covers a wide area
- In lots of different, cities and countries
- Uses equipment owned by the telecommunications companies
  - Expensive to build
  - Expensive to run

Network topologies

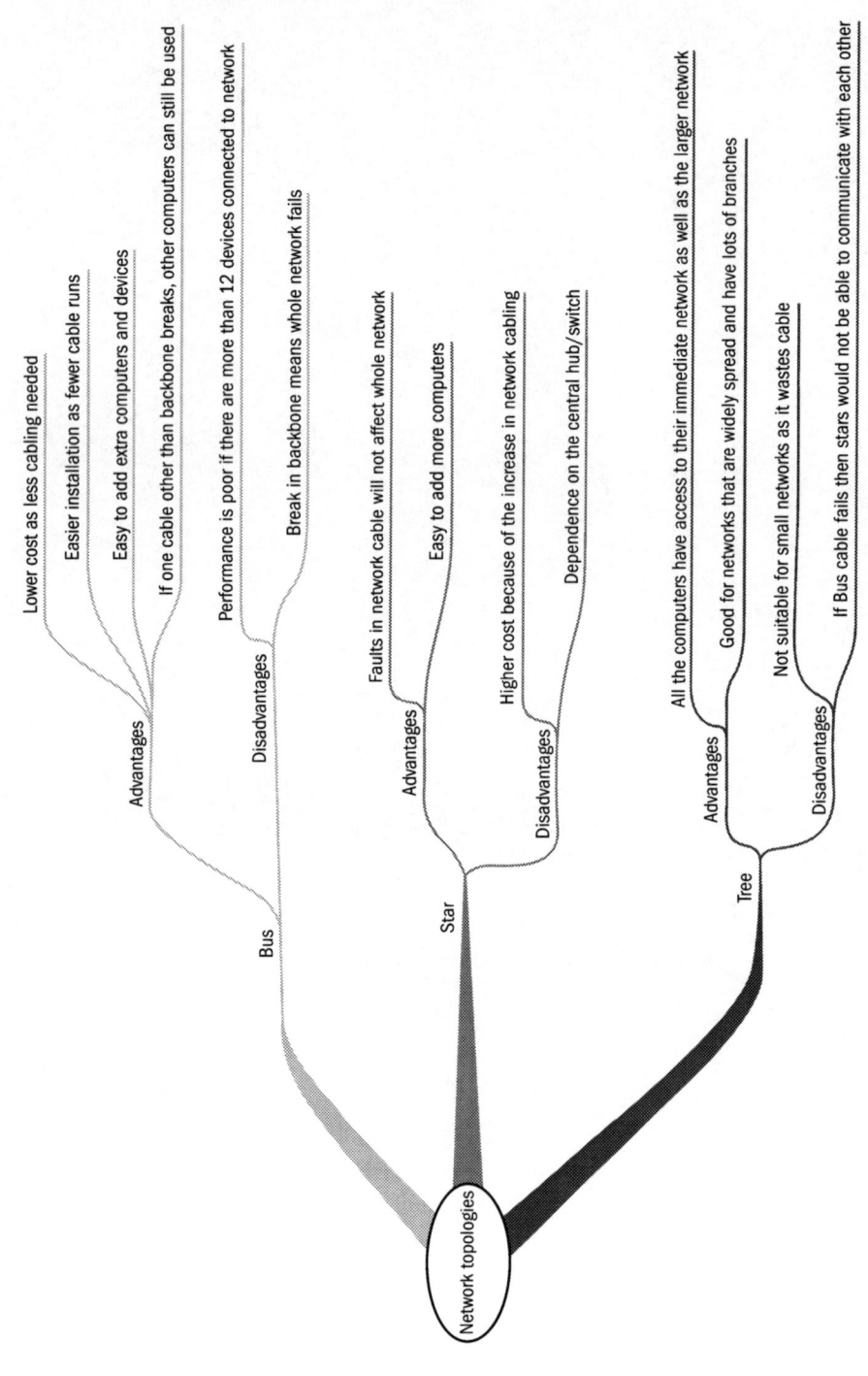

Network topologies

Bus

Advantages
- Lower cost as less cabling needed
- Easier installation as fewer cable runs
- Easy to add extra computers and devices
- If one cable other than backbone breaks, other computers can still be used

Disadvantages
- Performance is poor if there are more than 12 devices connected to network
- Break in backbone means whole network fails

Star

Advantages
- Faults in network cable will not affect whole network
- Easy to add more computers

Disadvantages
- Higher cost because of the increase in network cabling
- Dependence on the central hub/switch

Tree

Advantages
- All the computers have access to their immediate network as well as the larger network
- Good for networks that are widely spread and have lots of branches

Disadvantages
- Not suitable for small networks as it wastes cable
- If Bus cable fails then stars would not be able to communicate with each other

Advantages and disadvantages of networks

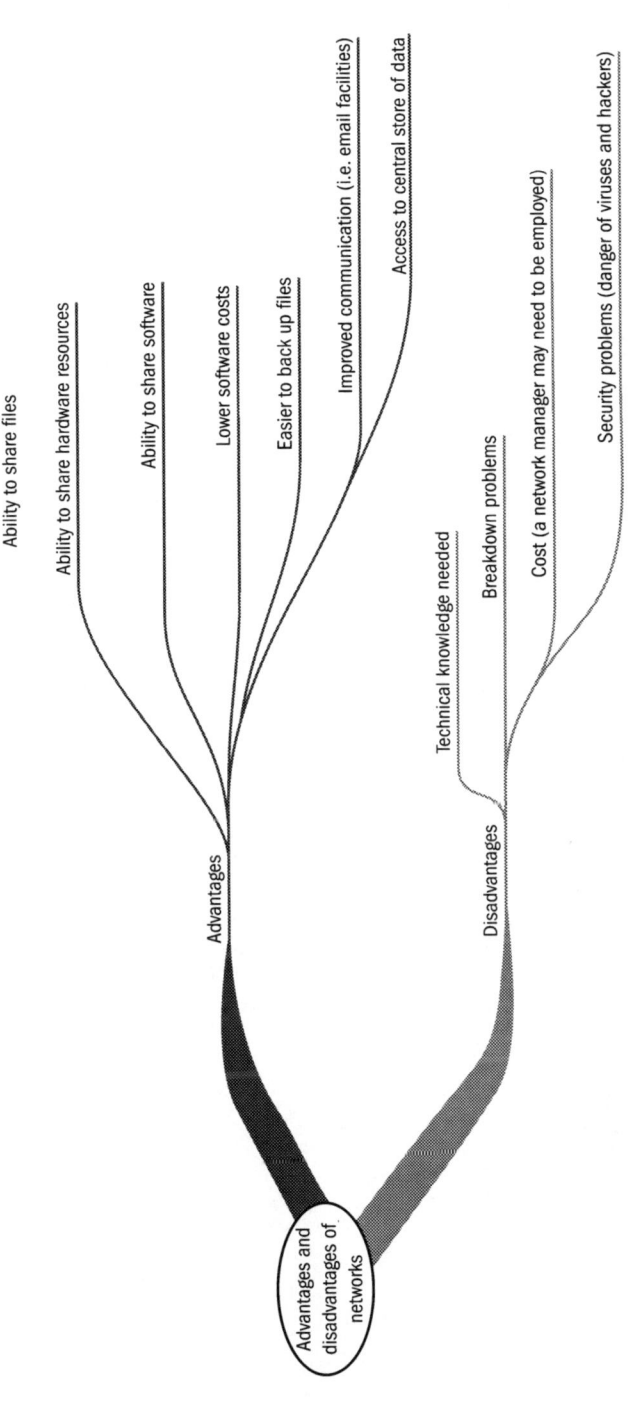

- Ability to share files
- Ability to share hardware resources
- Ability to share software
- Lower software costs
- Easier to back up files
- Improved communication (i.e. email facilities)
- Access to central store of data

Advantages

- Technical knowledge needed
- Breakdown problems
- Cost (a network manager may need to be employed)
- Security problems (danger of viruses and hackers)

Disadvantages

Advantages and disadvantages of networks

Videoconferencing

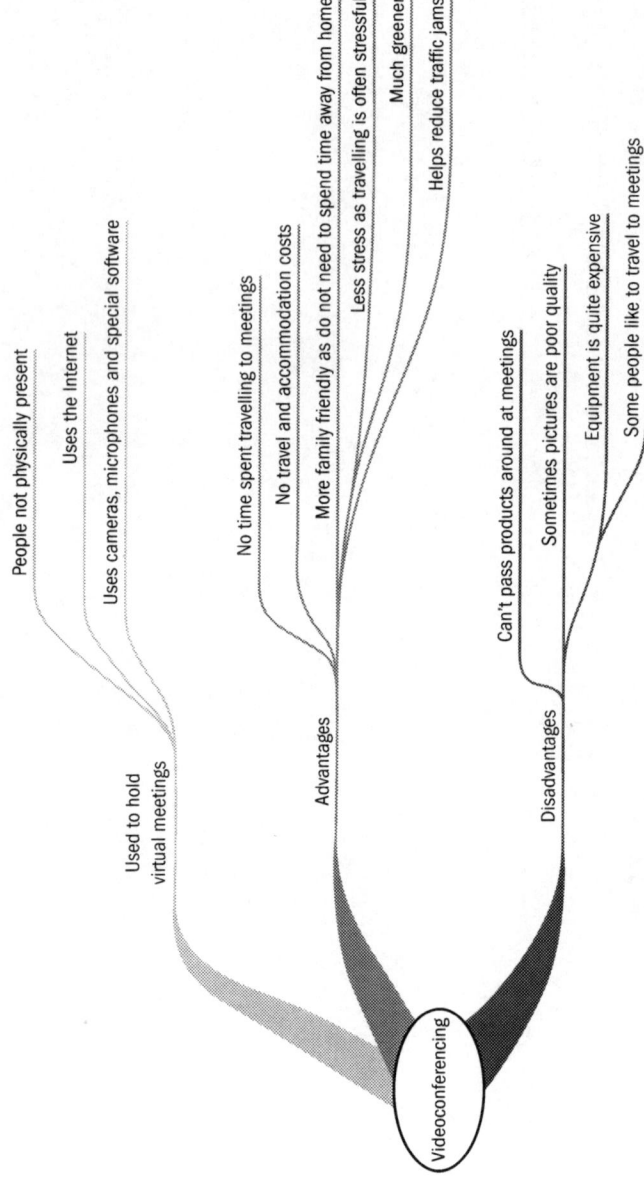

Videoconferencing

Used to hold virtual meetings
- People not physically present
- Uses the Internet
- Uses cameras, microphones and special software

Advantages
- No time spent travelling to meetings
- No travel and accommodation costs
- More family friendly as do not need to spend time away from home
- Less stress as travelling is often stressful
- Much greener
- Helps reduce traffic jams

Disadvantages
- Can't pass products around at meetings
- Sometimes pictures are poor quality
- Equipment is quite expensive
- Some people like to travel to meetings

ICT FOR IGCSE® TEACHER RESOURCE KIT © Oxford University Press 2012

Authentication techniques

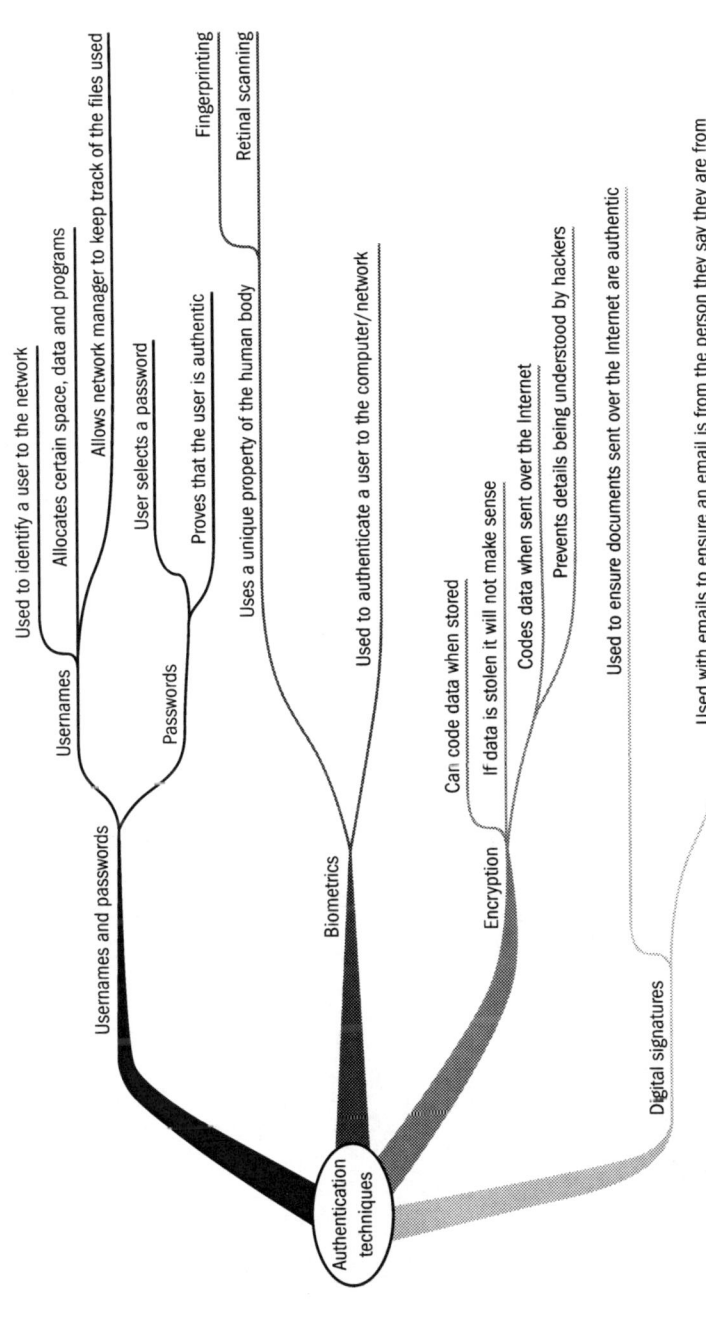

Authentication techniques

- Usernames and passwords
  - Usernames
    - Used to identify a user to the network
    - Allocates certain space, data and programs
    - Allows network manager to keep track of the files used
  - Passwords
    - User selects a password
    - Proves that the user is authentic
- Biometrics
  - Uses a unique property of the human body
    - Fingerprinting
    - Retinal scanning
  - Used to authenticate a user to the computer/network
- Encryption
  - Can code data when stored
  - If data is stolen it will not make sense
  - Codes data when sent over the Internet
  - Prevents details being understood by hackers
- Digital signatures
  - Used to ensure documents sent over the Internet are authentic
  - Used with emails to ensure an email is from the person they say they are from

Topic 5

Data types

Databases

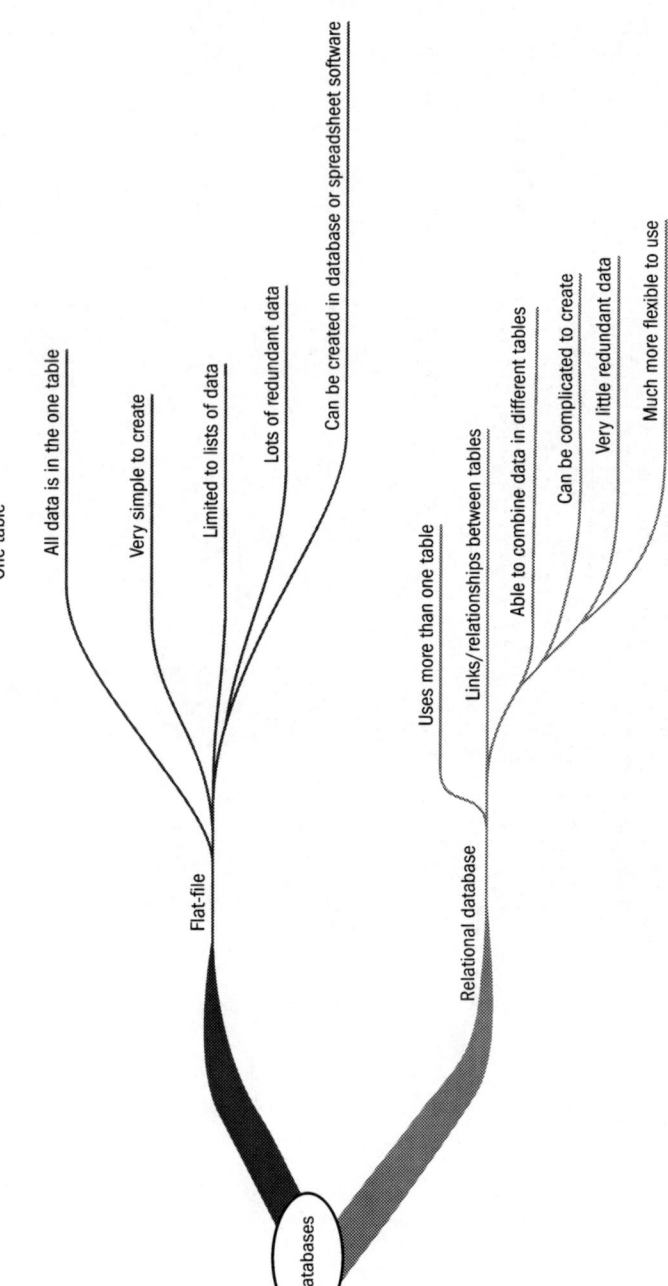

- Databases
  - Flat-file
    - One table
    - All data is in the one table
    - Very simple to create
    - Limited to lists of data
    - Lots of redundant data
    - Can be created in database or spreadsheet software
  - Relational database
    - Uses more than one table
    - Links/relationships between tables
    - Able to combine data in different tables
    - Can be complicated to create
    - Very little redundant data
    - Much more flexible to use

ICT FOR IGCSE® TEACHER RESOURCE KIT © Oxford University Press 2012

Topic 6

The effects of using ICT

Internet developments (Web 2.0 applications)

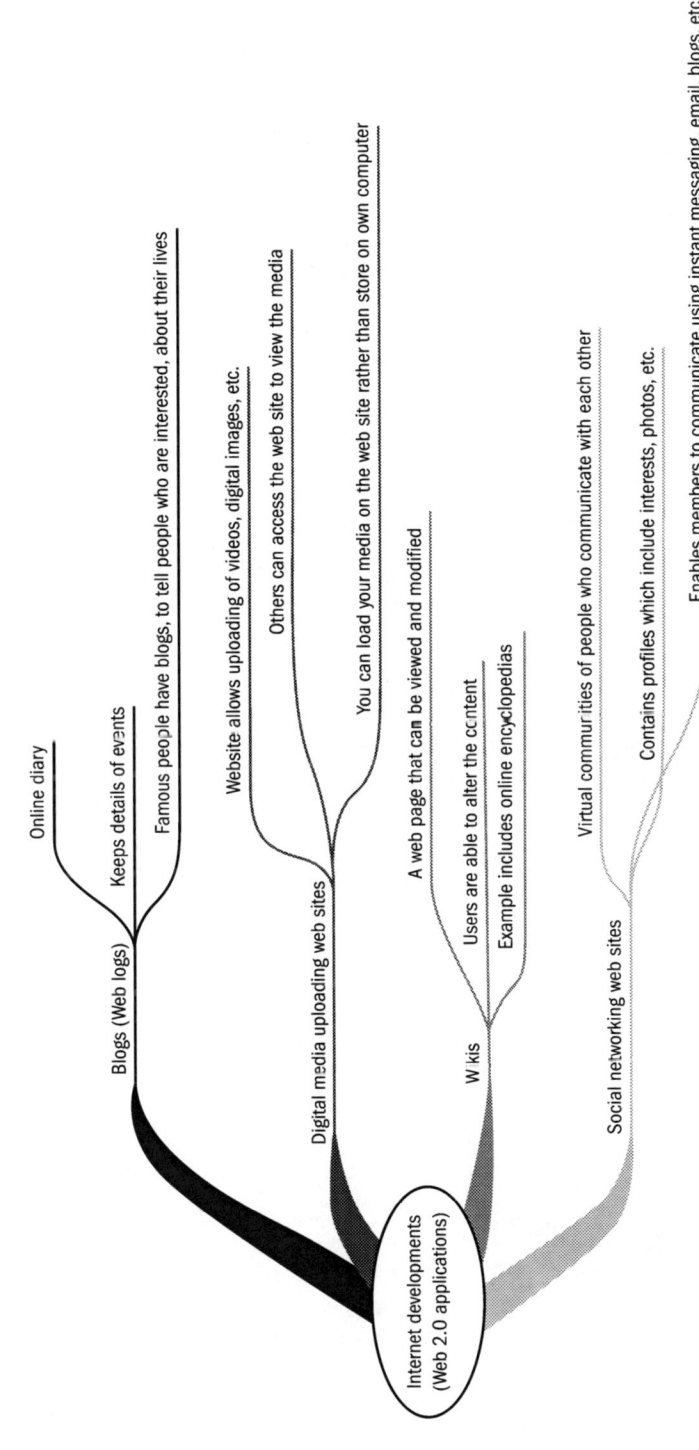

Online diary

Keeps details of events

Blogs (Web logs)

Famous people have blogs, to tell people who are interested, about their lives

Website allows uploading of videos, digital images, etc.

Others can access the web site to view the media

Digital media uploading web sites

You can load your media on the web site rather than store on own computer

A web page that can be viewed and modified

Users are able to alter the content

Wikis

Example includes online encyclopedias

Virtual communities of people who communicate with each other

Social networking web sites

Contains profiles which include interests, photos, etc.

Enables members to communicate using instant messaging, email, blogs, etc.

Internet developments (Web 2.0 applications)

Health hazards when using computers

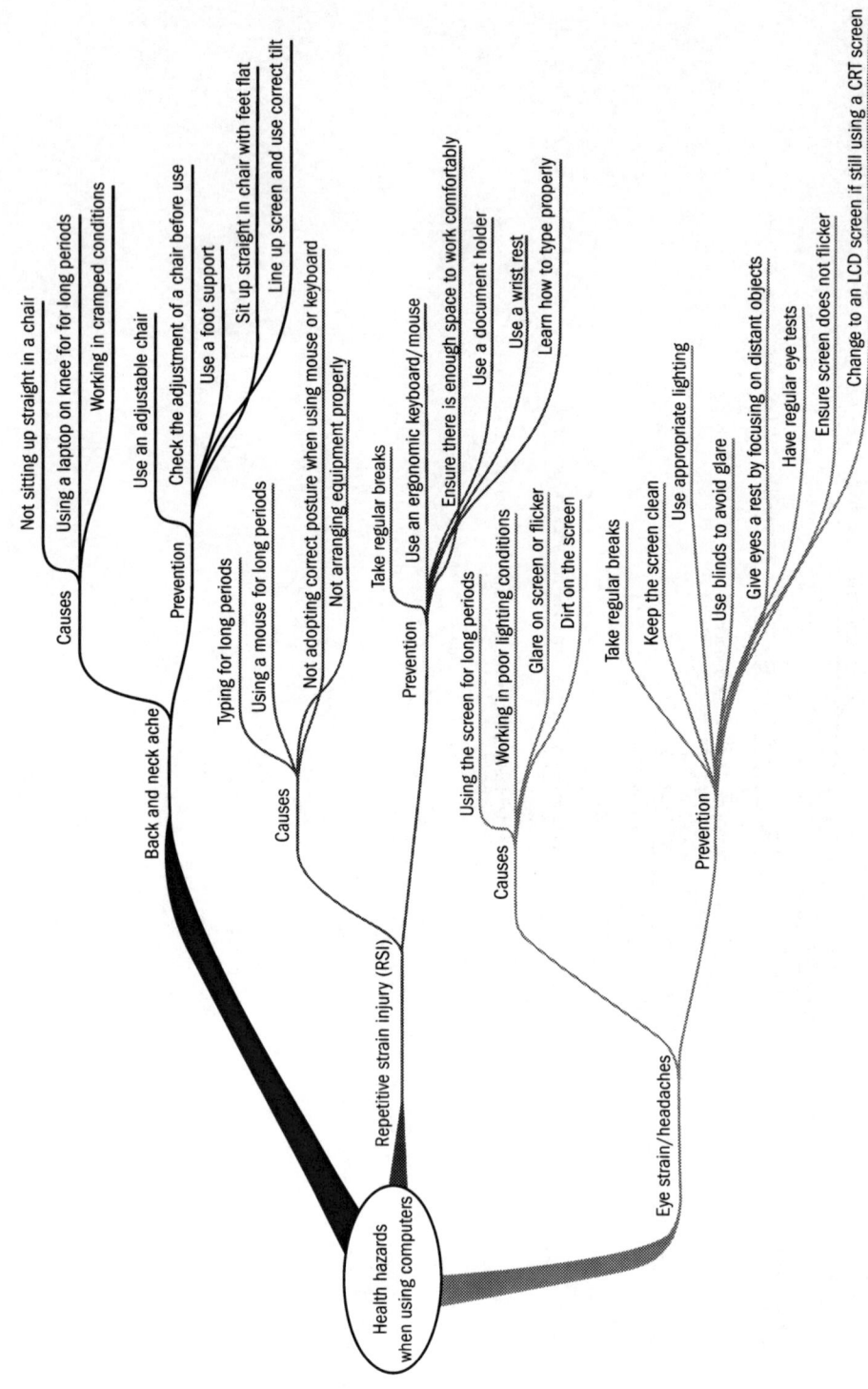

Safety issues

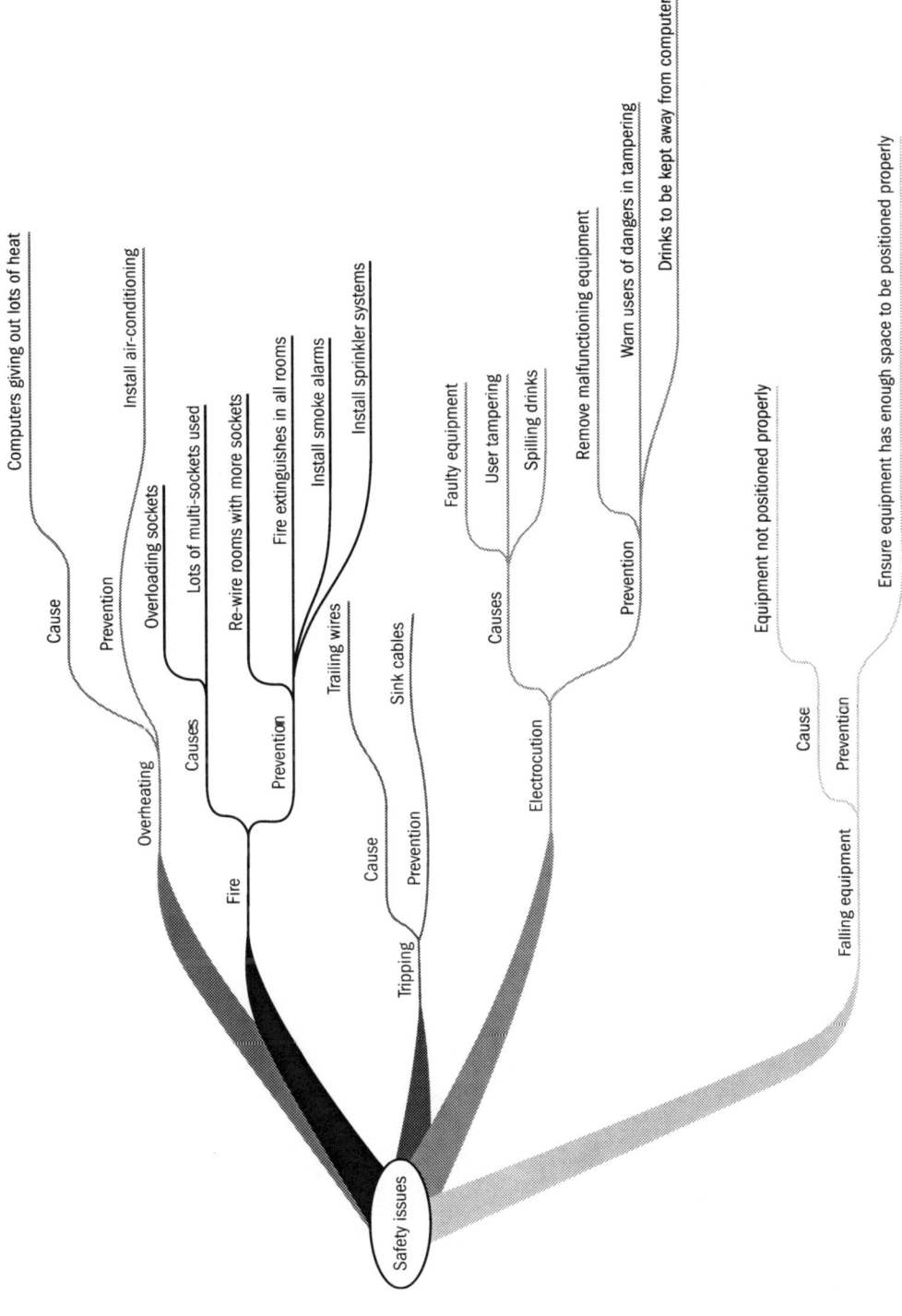

Safety issues

- Overheating
  - Cause
    - Computers giving out lots of heat
  - Prevention
    - Install air-conditioning
- Fire
  - Causes
    - Overloading sockets
  - Prevention
    - Lots of multi-sockets used
    - Re-wire rooms with more sockets
    - Fire extinguishes in all rooms
    - Install smoke alarms
    - Install sprinkler systems
- Tripping
  - Cause
    - Trailing wires
  - Prevention
    - Sink cables
- Electrocution
  - Causes
    - Faulty equipment
    - User tampering
    - Spilling drinks
  - Prevention
    - Remove malfunctioning equipment
    - Warn users of dangers in tampering
    - Drinks to be kept away from computers
- Falling equipment
  - Cause
    - Equipment not positioned properly
  - Prevention
    - Ensure equipment has enough space to be positioned properly

Protecting data against viruses and other deliberate damage

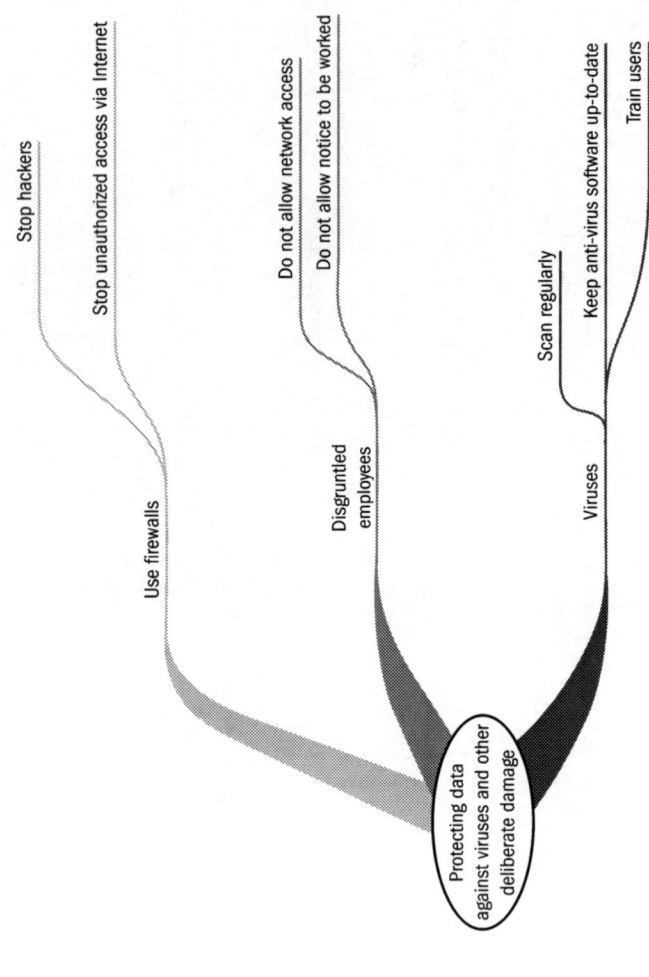

Stop hackers

Stop unauthorized access via Internet

Do not allow network access

Do not allow notice to be worked

Keep anti-virus software up-to-date

Train users

Scan regularly

Use firewalls

Disgruntled employees

Viruses

Protecting data against viruses and other deliberate damage

ICT FOR IGCSE® TEACHER RESOURCE KIT   © Oxford University Press 2012

Protecting stored or transmitted data from unauthorized access

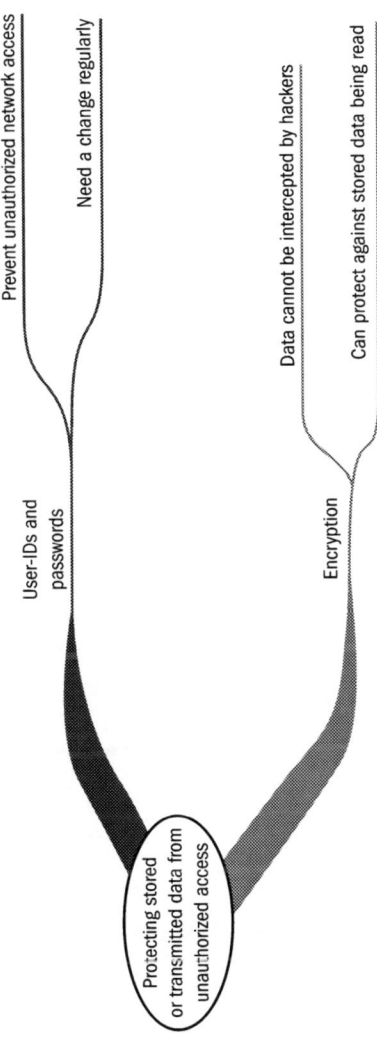

Use of blogs

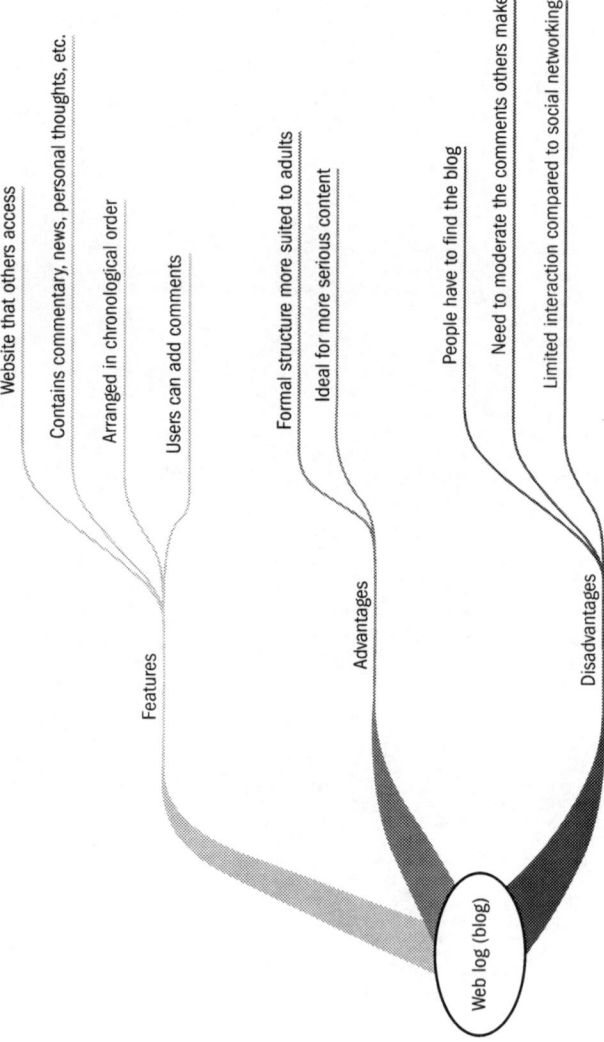

- Features
  - Website that others access
  - Contains commentary, news, personal thoughts, etc.
  - Arranged in chronological order
  - Users can add comments
- Advantages
  - Formal structure more suited to adults
  - Ideal for more serious content
- Disadvantages
  - People have to find the blog
  - Need to moderate the comments others make
  - Limited interaction compared to social networking

Web log (blog)

ICT FOR IGCSE® TEACHER RESOURCE KIT   © Oxford University Press 2012

Topic 7

The ways in which ICT is used

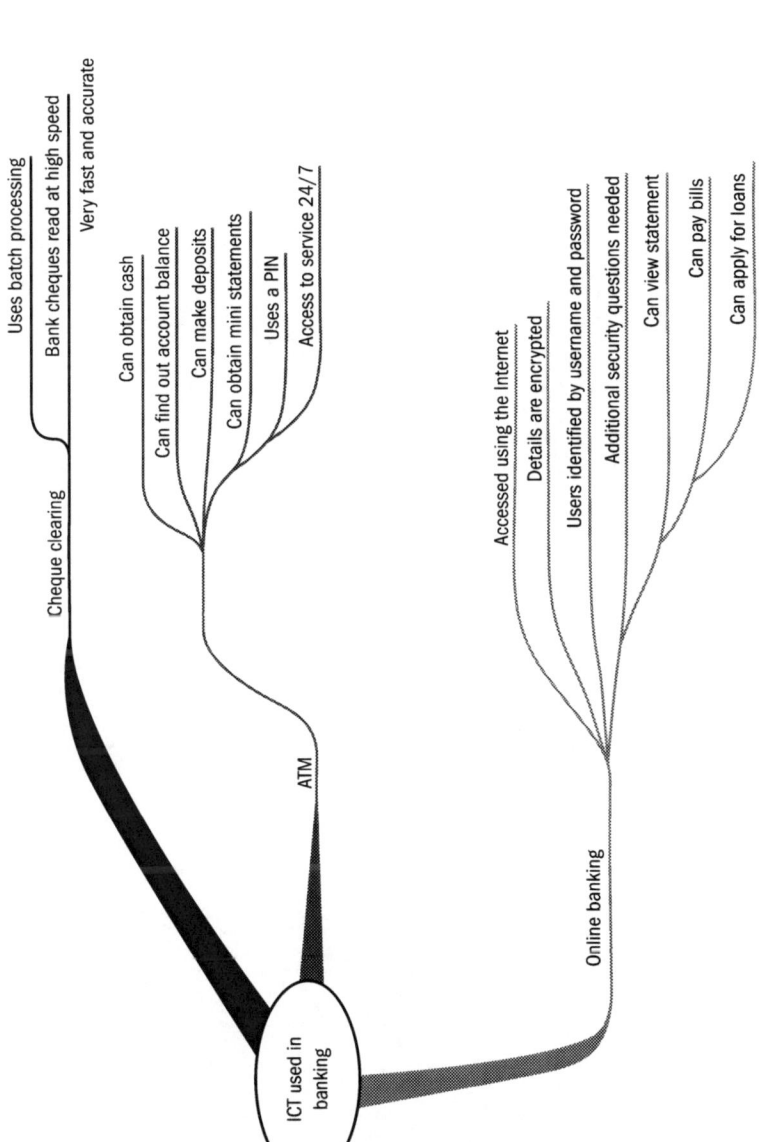

ICT used in banking

ICT used in banking

Cheque clearing
- Uses batch processing
- Bank cheques read at high speed
- Very fast and accurate

ATM
- Can obtain cash
- Can find out account balance
- Can make deposits
- Can obtain mini statements
- Uses a PIN
- Access to service 24/7

Online banking
- Accessed using the Internet
- Details are encrypted
- Users identified by username and password
- Additional security questions needed
- Can view statement
- Can pay bills
- Can apply for loans

Data logging

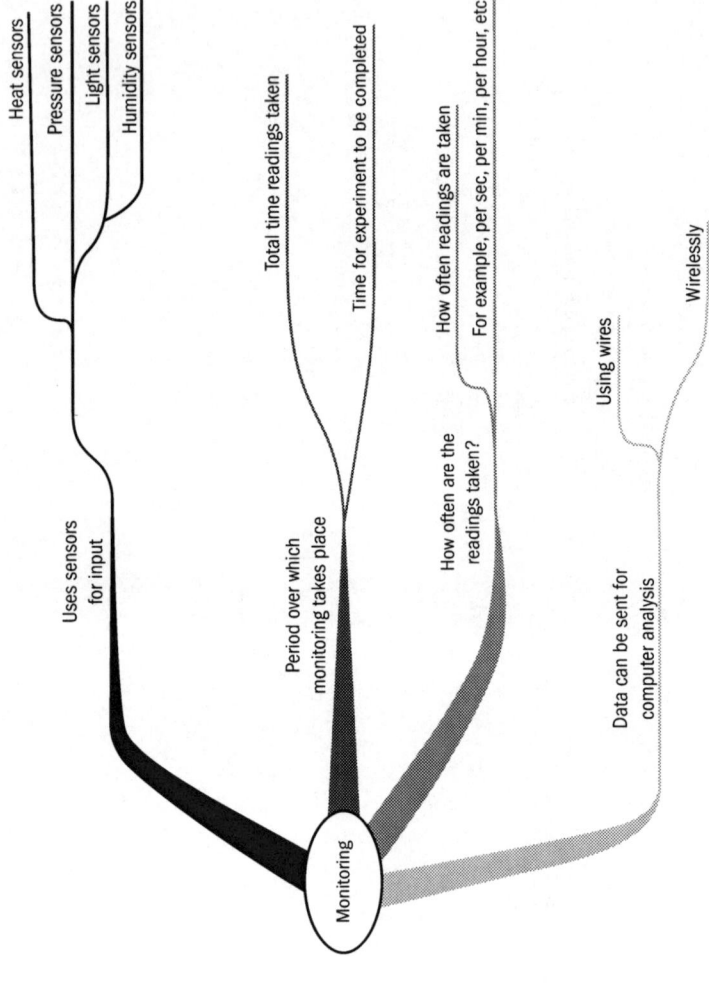

- Uses sensors for input
  - Heat sensors
  - Pressure sensors
  - Light sensors
  - Humidity sensors

Monitoring

- Period over which monitoring takes place
  - Total time readings taken
  - Time for experiment to be completed
- How often are the readings taken?
  - How often readings are taken
  - For example, per sec, per min, per hour, etc.
- Data can be sent for computer analysis
  - Using wires
  - Wirelessly

ICT FOR IGCSE® TEACHER RESOURCE KIT   © Oxford University Press 2012

Expert systems

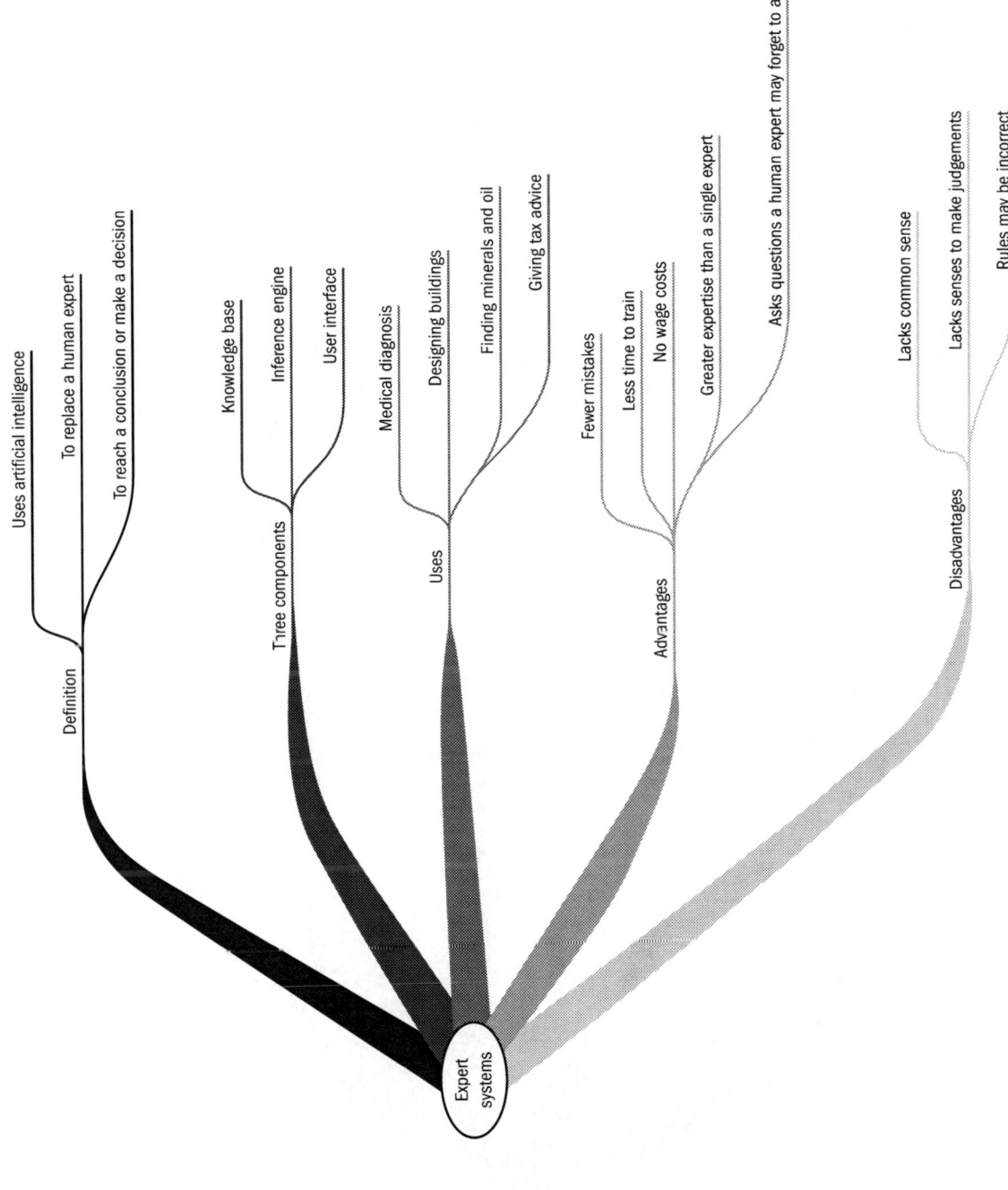

Expert systems

Definition
- Uses artificial intelligence
- To replace a human expert
- To reach a conclusion or make a decision

Three components
- Knowledge base
- Inference engine
- User interface

Uses
- Medical diagnosis
- Designing buildings
- Finding minerals and oil
- Giving tax advice

Advantages
- Fewer mistakes
- Less time to train
- No wage costs
- Greater expertise than a single expert
- Asks questions a human expert may forget to ask

Disadvantages
- Lacks common sense
- Lacks senses to make judgements
- Rules may be incorrect

Topic 8

System analysis and design

The systems life cycle

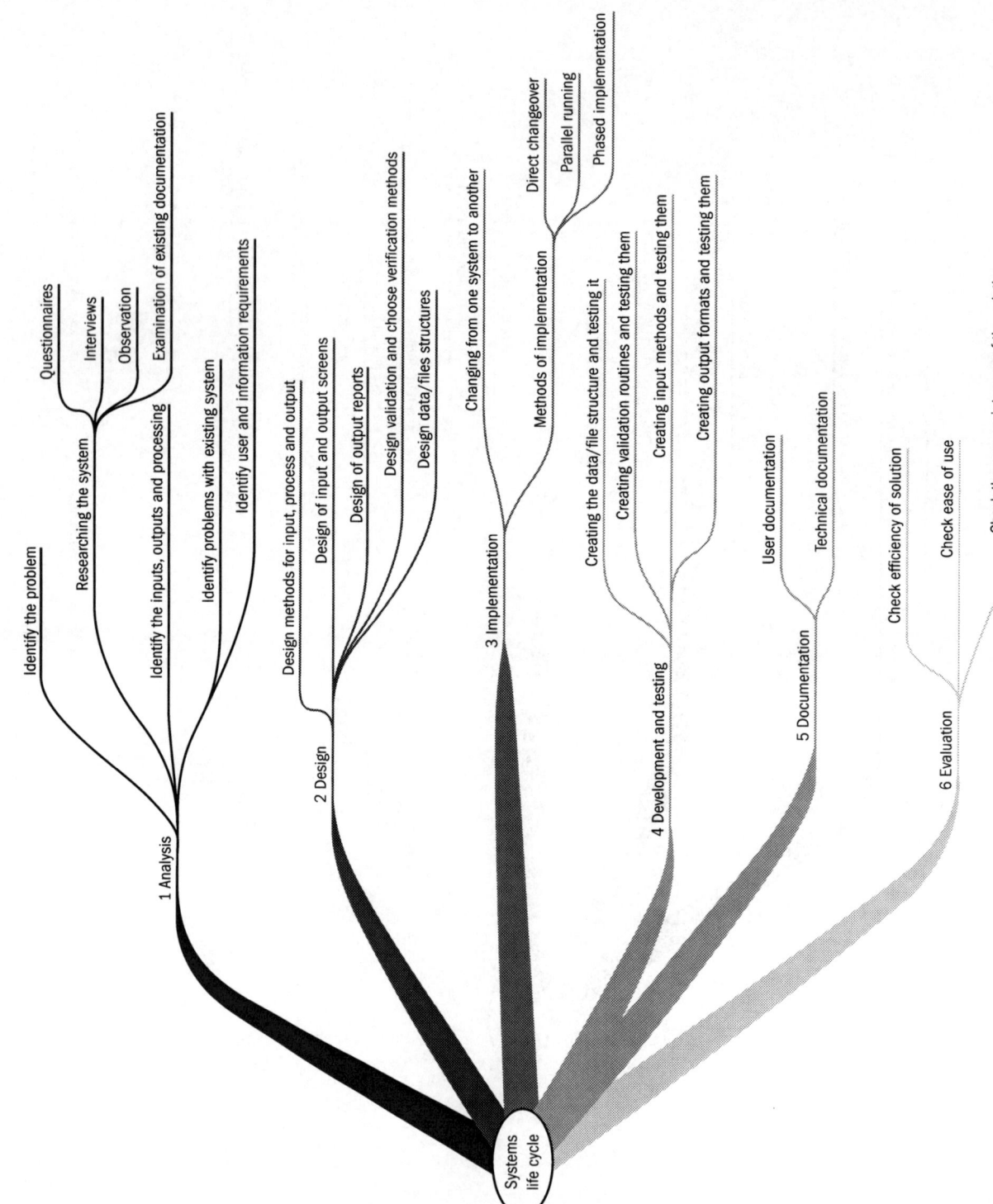

ICT FOR IGCSE® TEACHER RESOURCE KIT   © Oxford University Press 2012

Changeover methods

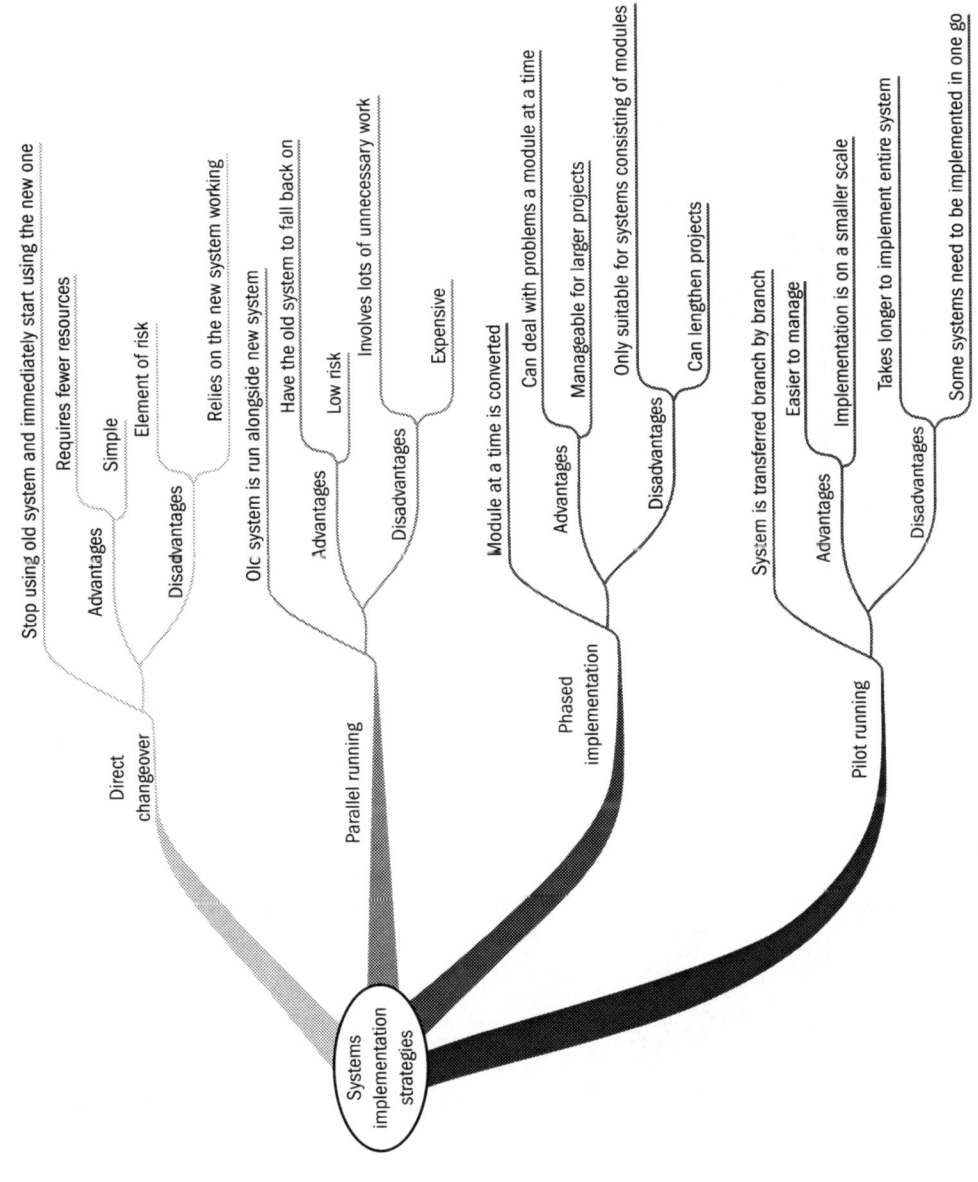

Systems implementation strategies

- **Direct changeover**
  - Stop using old system and immediately start using the new one
  - **Advantages**
    - Requires fewer resources
    - Simple
  - **Disadvantages**
    - Element of risk
    - Relies on the new system working

- **Parallel running**
  - Old system is run alongside new system
  - **Advantages**
    - Have the old system to fall back on
    - Low risk
  - **Disadvantages**
    - Involves lots of unnecessary work
    - Expensive

- **Phased implementation**
  - Module at a time is converted
  - **Advantages**
    - Can deal with problems a module at a time
    - Manageable for larger projects
  - **Disadvantages**
    - Only suitable for systems consisting of modules
    - Can lengthen projects

- **Pilot running**
  - System is transferred branch by branch
  - **Advantages**
    - Easier to manage
    - Implementation is on a smaller scale
  - **Disadvantages**
    - Takes longer to implement entire system
    - Some systems need to be implemented in one go

Test plans

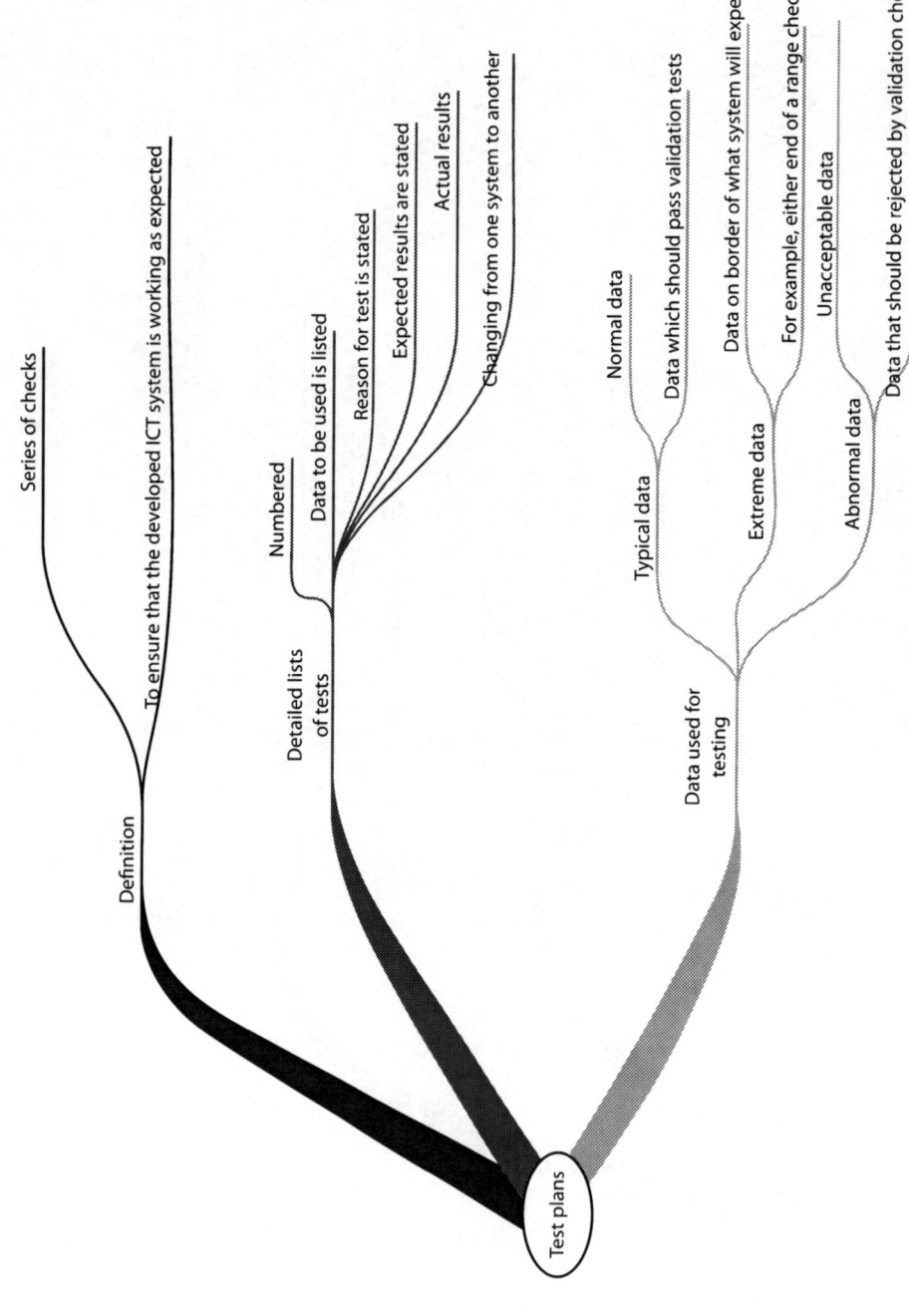

- Definition
  - Series of checks
  - To ensure that the developed ICT system is working as expected

- Detailed lists of tests
  - Numbered
    - Data to be used is listed
  - Reason for test is stated
  - Expected results are stated
  - Actual results
  - Changing from one system to another

- Data used for testing
  - Typical data
    - Normal data
    - Data which should pass validation tests
  - Extreme data
    - Data on border of what system will expect
    - For example, either end of a range check
  - Abnormal data
    - Unacceptable data
    - Data that should be rejected by validation checks

Test plans

ICT FOR IGCSE® TEACHER RESOURCE KIT © Oxford University Press 2012

Topic 9

Communication

Email facilities

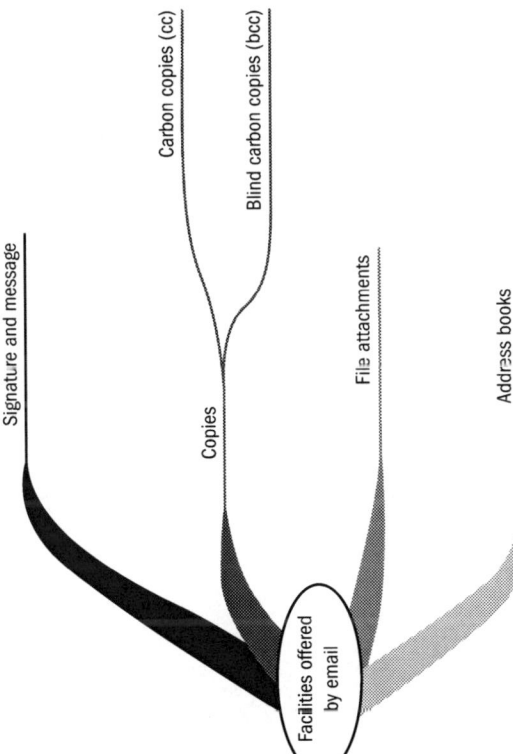

Advantages and disadvantages of email

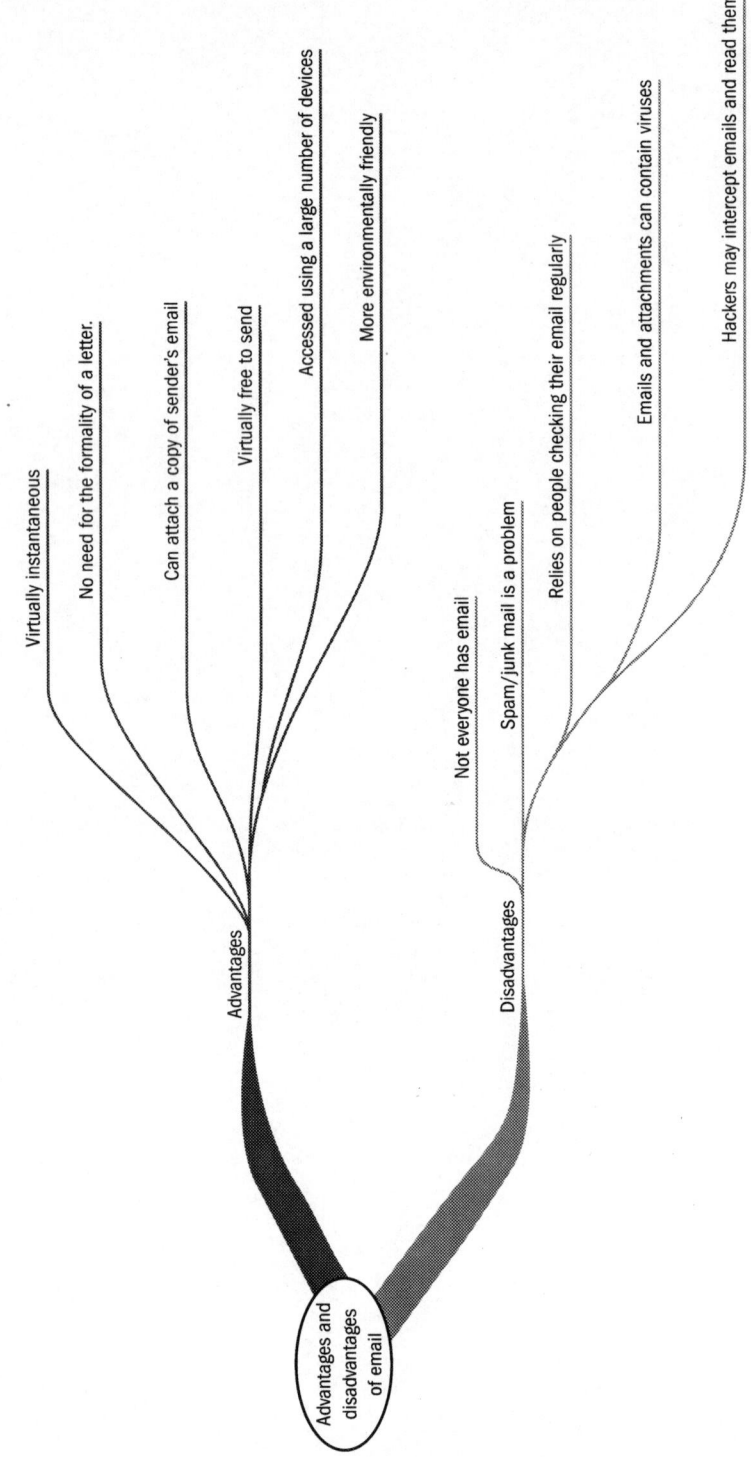

- Advantages
  - Virtually instantaneous
  - No need for the formality of a letter.
  - Can attach a copy of sender's email
  - Virtually free to send
  - Accessed using a large number of devices
  - More environmentally friendly
- Disadvantages
  - Not everyone has email
  - Spam/junk mail is a problem
  - Relies on people checking their email regularly
  - Emails and attachments can contain viruses
  - Hackers may intercept emails and read them

Advantages and disadvantages of email

ICT FOR IGCSE® TEACHER RESOURCE KIT